# TROUBLE
## AT THE
# TABLE

# TROUBLE AT THE TABLE

## Gathering the Tribes for Worship

## Carol Doran & Thomas H. Troeger

Abingdon Press
*Nashville*

TROUBLE AT THE TABLE

*This book is printed on recycled, acid-free paper.*

**Library of Congress Cataloging-in-Publication Data**

Doran, Carol.
   Trouble at the table : gathering the tribes for worship / Carol Doran and Thomas H. Troeger.
      p.   cm.
   Includes bibliographical references.
   ISBN 0-687-42656-1 (alk. paper)
   1. Public worship.   2. Church music   I. Troeger. Thomas H.,
1945–     . II. Title.
BV15.D6738      1992
264'.001—dc20
                                                                      92–20502
                                                                      CIP

Lines from "Music Swims Back to Me," on p. 66, by Anne Sexton. From *To Bedlam and Part Way Back* by Anne Sexton. Copyright © 1960 by Anne Sexton. Reprinted by permission of Houghton Mifflin Co. All rights reserved.

"Pastor, Lead Our Circle Dance," on pp. 154–55, by Carol Doran and Thomas H. Troeger. From *New Hymns for the Life of the Church*. Copyright © 1990 by Oxford University Press, Inc. Reprinted by permission.

Scripture quotations, unless otherwise noted, are from the New Revised Standard Version of the Bible, copyright 1989 by the Division of Christian Education of the National Council of the Churches of Christ in the USA. Used by permission.

Those noted REB are from *The Revised English Bible*. Copyright © 1989 by the Delegates of the Oxford University Press and The Syndics of the Cambridge University Press. Reprinted by permission.

MANUFACTURED IN THE UNITED STATES OF AMERICA

*To pastors, musicians, and lay leaders who have explored in our classes and workshops the ideas and principles of this book and who share with us a vision of the church unified and empowered by the glad and faithful worship of God*

# CONTENTS

# Chapter 3: Maps and Images
## Giving Shape to the Yearnings of the Heart...............93

# Chapter 4: Strategies for Change
## Working with the Tribes...............................137

# PREFACE

If we were standing before you to lead a workshop on revitalizing worship, you would see that we are two different individuals. You would hear two voices, and through their separate sounds you would sense that we each talk in a distinctive way about the task of revitalizing worship. But reading our words on the page creates the illusion that there is a single author, and sometimes when one of us tells a personal story, you may wonder, "Who is speaking now?"

I, Carol Doran, am a pastoral musician, who began my career as a young person playing the piano in the Sunday school services of the church in which I grew up. I went on to study music professionally and to serve churches as organist and choir director. For seventeen years, I have been teaching in a theological seminary in Rochester, New York, leading music in daily worship services, directing the chapel choir, developing the Pastoral Music program, and working with denominations and musical groups throughout North America in developing the vitality of their worship.

I, Tom Troeger, am a preacher and a teacher of preachers, who has given special attention to the development of the religious imagination as a source of spiritual renewal and theological insight for the proclamation of the gospel.

Although I now teach in Denver, Colorado, I worked for fourteen years with Carol, developing the seminary chapel program in Rochester, teaching courses on worship, and leading workshops around the country.

This book represents what we have learned from planning and leading hundreds of services together, from our collaboration as poet and composer in the creation of new hymns, and from our working with clergy, musicians, seminary students, lay leaders, denominational groups, and congregations. These have included rural, suburban, and city congregations, churches of every size, many different ethnic groups, persons with a wide spectrum of theological belief, traditionalists and innovators, those excited about their liturgical life and those who are discouraged.

As I, Carol, and I, Tom, speak to you from these pages, we hope that you will hear not only our voices, but also the voices of the faithful people who have told us about the joys and challenges of their liturgical life. The goal that drew them to our courses and workshops is the goal of this book: to bring the worship of God closer to the best intentions and the highest visions of their hearts.

Carol Doran
Colgate Rochester Divinity School
Bexley Hall/Crozer Theological Seminary

Thomas H. Troeger
Iliff School of Theology

February, 1992

# CHAPTER

# Trouble at the Table
### *The Crisis in Worship*

It was the first fine, sweet day of spring. Tired of the stale winter air in my office, I (Tom) left the seminary where I teach and walked across the street to the park. There I could sit on my favorite bench and listen to bird song, the splash of the fountain in the reservoir, and the wind in the trees.

No sooner had I sat down than a young couple arrived carrying guitars. They began serenading each other with folk songs. A few minutes later another couple settled on the grass behind me with a radio the size of a suitcase, which they tuned to the local classical station. Then some college students came along and tossed a Frisbee to country western music. Finally, a van drove up and parked in front of me. It featured a bumper sticker: "I'm a Hard Rocker." The sticker was not necessary.

Bird song, splashing water, and the wind in the trees were lost to colliding rhythms and a general cacophonous rumble. I felt surrounded by alien tribes: the folk tribe, the classical tribe, the country western tribe, and the hard rock tribe. Each group turned up its volume as the others arrived so that staying near the source of their sound, they did not have to listen to the competition.

For a moment I considered going around and asking them all to turn off their music. But I knew how effective that would be! As a private citizen, I had no recognizable authority to speak up for the birds, the fountain, and the trees.

So I got up and walked away, but as the great cacophony of musical tribes faded in the distance, there arose in my mind the memory of all the different kinds of music that members of congregations want sung in church.

Paul Westermeyer has given a vivid description of the great variety of demands from the various tribes in our local congregations:

> Some people want gospel hymns, some want rock, some want Lutheran chorales, still others don't want to sing at all and expect the choir to do it. Some want the choir to sing 16th-century motets, others want it to sing only 19th-century music. One group wants non-sexist texts when referring to humanity; others want non-sexist terms for both humanity and God; others insist one should never alter the original text.[1]

Each group holds its particular style of praise as precious and sacred, as the one that most effectively releases the prayer that is in their hearts.

What about your church? If it is like most churches these days, it is indeed a gathering of various tribes with different tastes and ideas and feelings about worship. It has not always been like this. Our memories take us back to times when churches seemed to have a unified idea of how their own denomination's church music should sound. The "old" hymnals, which now languish in a Sunday school closet, are tangible records that the boundaries of that style were as firm as the book's outside covers. Was it not just a few years ago that everyone seemed content with what "we've always done"? We dream about the serenity of those simpler times. We cannot help longing for the unanimity of opinion about worship practice, which we imagine has pervaded Judeo-Christian history.

This is not, however, the first time that the community of faith has faced the challenge of drawing together many different tribes in the common worship of God. The psalmist tells us about the hill in Jerusalem where

> . . . the tribes go up,
>     the tribes of the LORD . . .
>     to give thanks to the name of the LORD.
>                                         (Psalm 122:4)

Commentators have remarked that we do not know if the psalmist is describing "actual or idealized practice."[2] Perhaps we will never know for sure, but there are sound reasons for believing that the tribes did not get along all that well. Like the various groups in our churches, they brought to the praise of God a wide range of preferences and practices.

Technically speaking, a tribe is a primary kinship unit. We are extending the term to cover any group that is drawn together by common interests, values, and goals. The fans for the hometown team, the students of a charismatic teacher, the devoted audience of a pop singer, people passionately committed to a social cause, a prayer and fellowship circle, the choir, the Sunday school staff—all are tribes of one sort or another. Some are joined by enduring bonds, others by passing fashion.

## Worship Reformers as Heirs of King David

We feel most comfortable when we are with our own tribe. We know its customs, its peculiar character and allegiances, its beliefs and rituals, its symbols and code

13

words, its particular ways of celebrating and being together.

Scholars have helped us to see that these characteristics marked the tribes of Israel. For centuries the tribes lived relatively separate from each other, maintaining their distinctive identities, and only joining forces to provide for their mutual defense through a loose confederation known as an amphictyony.

It was King David who focused their common interests. He brought them together by the power of his charisma and by moving the ark of the covenant, the most sacred symbol of their worship, to Jerusalem. Those of us who are responsible for finding ways to bring our diverse congregations together around the central symbols of our faith are heirs to the tradition of King David.

David contributed to the liturgical life of his community's faith in at least four ways:

1. Through his poetic and musical gifts, which he used to supply the congregation with hymns (psalms) of extraordinary power and beauty.

2. Through Spirit-filled liturgical dance.

3. Through his perceptive understanding of the power of symbols as evidenced in his use of the ark to bring together the tribes.

4. By envisioning the building of a temple where the tribes could join together in the worship of God.

It is important to note that in two of these matters he met resistance. Michal, Saul's daughter, severely chastised him for his joyful liturgical dance, and God through the prophet Nathan indicated that it was not yet time to build the temple.

As heirs of David's ministry of worship leadership, we find themes in his story that appear again and again in the history of renewing the church's corporate prayer. His example reminds us to use all our gifts in drawing together the tribes of our congregation, but at the same time to be ready to face resistance and disappointment. Not everything David tried to do in leading worship was accepted by all of the people, and not everything he envisioned came to pass in his lifetime.

Even the things David accomplished did not last forever. The relationship among the tribes was always tenuous because although their "boundaries disappeared during the Monarchy, the tribal concept of pioneer days persisted."[3] As a result, David's unification did not hold up for long. His son Solomon built the temple and in almost no time after Solomon's death the old tribal allegiances and geographic loyalties reasserted themselves.

## Tribal Behavior in Our Churches

We are familiar with how this ancient phenomenon continues in new forms in our churches and denominations today. During the last fourteen years of working with worshiping communities in the United States and Canada, we recall many stories of "tribes" asserting themselves in ways that entangled, strained, and sometimes broke the community apart.

We now tell a few of these stories to help you remember your own. We encourage you to draw upon your experience as a resource for trying out the principles and practices that we will be presenting. The object is not simply to remember "when things went wrong," but rather to analyze the causes so that your future liturgical leadership can be more effective.

Our stories include several kinds of worshiping communities, from a national meeting to regional conferences to a local parish. The range of examples makes it clear that the challenge of gathering the tribes involves forces in church and society that are greater than our individual

15

local situations. Although every community has its distinctive character, what we face in any particular situation is often a manifestation of these larger forces. That realization may initially make our task seem overwhelming, but it also encourages our work by reminding us that we are not just tinkering with this or that idea for Sunday's worship. We are engaged with issues of profound importance to the future of life and faith: how will we lead the church to worship God in a way that draws on the best of what each tribe has to offer without reinforcing the fragmentation and the struggle for domination that characterize our culture?

## A Story of Two Tribes Divided by a Hymn

We were at the opening service of a national meeting. The liturgy had been planned by a group of people who are familiar with the tradition represented by most of the participants, including the divisions that mark most of their local parishes. Many elements of the service would turn out to be excellent, but the first line of the opening hymn was "I praise you God for the wonder of myself." Note the personal and reflexive pronouns: "I," "myself."

Discussions after the service revealed that there were at least two tribes in great conflict during the singing of the piece. One was a tribe who expected that the beginning of worship would not focus on themselves, but on God, and that the expression of praise and glory would involve a sound that was richer than the plucked strings of a guitar. The other was the group who found a rare opportunity through this song (that had been specially commissioned for the occasion) to acknowledge the value of individuals who have faithful ministries in the church, but are seldom publicly recognized for their gifts and talents.

At a reception that followed the service, it was difficult for members of the different tribes to converse with each other because neither was theologically articulate about their differences. With the exception of a few people who identified the narcissism of the text or the thinness of the accompaniment, most people reduced their response to assertions of individual taste: "I liked it." "I didn't like it."

## A Story of Tribes Divided by Politics

We recall talking with a historian of worship from another seminary who loved his tradition yet was not opposed to innovation. Nevertheless, he and the rest of the community had come to a point of deciding to attend worship solely on the basis of which tribe was leading the service that day. In his words: "Worship has been entirely politicized. . . . You often come out feeling more guilty and immobilized than when you went in." Grace, reconciliation, shared faith, tradition, a sense of the transcendent—all had bowed to the immediate concern and experience of whichever tribe was supposedly responsible for leading the worship of the whole community.

## A Story of Tribes Divided Over the Purpose of Worship

A denominational group once invited us in as consultants because they felt, to quote their invitation, "a crisis in our spiritual life." This broadly stated symptom was more precisely identified when we met with them, and one member explained that they were always being asked to break into small groups to talk about their feelings and concerns. The tribe that had authority to prepare the services thought of worship as primarily "sharing and caring," and they completely ignored another tribe that wanted to sing some of their great hymns and offer their traditional prayers.

## A Story of Rootless Tribes

A local congregation invited us to meet with their worship committee under the general injunction of feeling a need to "revitalize [their] worship." But upon meeting with them, we discovered that they had no clear idea of what that might mean. When we asked what held them together as a group, one of their leaders said, "Our liberalism." However, subsequent conversation showed that one person's definition of liberalism was not another's, and that the assumption of a general liberal stance crumbled when they talked candidly about their views.

We asked what were the historical strengths of their tradition, and they acknowledged that they did not know. It was like talking to a tribe that had lost whatever had once bound it together, so that the members wandered rootlessly on their own.

## Touching Off Tribal Warfare with Autocratic Leadership

The tribal warfare recorded in these stories often originates in the behavior of the leaders. They may be acting with the best of intentions, but the unexamined assumptions of their liturgical decisions give their leadership the appearance of insensitivity to other customs and understandings.

It is, for example, easy to assume that what we know and love about worship will most effectively express the prayer of the entire congregation. We have seen this happen again and again as people choose music "because it is my favorite" or organize the ritual according to "the way we did in the church where I grew up." This is not to say that the musical selection or the structure of the ritual is necessarily inappropriate. What concerns us is the facile manner in which it is assumed that the leader's personal experience is an adequate standard of judgment for the congregation's corporate prayer.

A common form of such autocratic behavior is printing only the words of a hymn and assuming "everyone knows the tune." In an age when most churches have people from a wide range of backgrounds, such an assumption is nearly always unwarranted. A person from another tribe will be left out of that act of musical prayer, and the lack of hospitality will initiate or increase his or her sense of being an outsider, a stranger to the community's praise.

Another form of autocratic behavior is springing something new on people without adequate preparation. We think of people who have decided to serve communion in a new way without discussion and preparation of the servers or the congregation ahead of time. Because it is clear in the leader's head, she or he assumes it is clear to everyone else. But in matters of holy ritual people's anxiety about "doing it right" is usually so high that any change requires careful preparation and rehearsal.

Yet another common form of liturgical surprise is to spring a new piece of music on the musician without time for its preparation. The musician does not want to encounter unexpected key changes or to have inadequate time to prepare registrations on the organ that do not match the character of the words and music. To present the music in the most effective way will take time and practice.

Note that in these examples the leader may not intend to put the communion servers or the musician in an awkward position, but the facile assumption that "everybody knows it" results in behavior that comes across to others as insensitive to their part in the worship of God. Leaders increase the tribal conflict if they act without examining the assumptions that lie behind their choices and judgments.

## The Temptation to Abdicate Leadership

Sometimes in the effort to avoid the pitfalls of acting autocratically and in hope that the conflict will disappear, leaders abdicate their role. Their denomination has supplied them with hymnals and liturgical resources that are rich with materials for revitalizing their worship, but the threat of conflict and resistance is enough to paralyze them. It is easier to keep choosing from the same limited selection of congregational songs and to keep the same ritual form than to invest the time and energy required to introduce and lead new material effectively.

We think here of a congregation that was getting ready to celebrate Pentecost entirely within the confines of its well-established hymnody, not allowing an opening for the Holy Spirit to come in fresh ways as it did upon the early church (Acts 2). The preacher and most of the planning committee were willing to abdicate their role of supporting anything new, but not the musician.

She had found a different form of congregational music from the ecumenical community of Taizé. She introduced to the planning group a piece that consisted of a prayer refrain in which the only words were "Veni Sancte Spiritus" (Come, Holy Spirit). The congregation's repeated singing of this phrase was to be interwoven with vocal solos and instrumental descants. Working with the committee, the musician got all of them excited about what a beautiful prelude this would make for the Pentecost service. The preacher even drew on the committee's experience with the musician to illustrate his sermon on the Holy Spirit. The result was a moving service in which the traditional hymns had a greater impact than ever before because the music from Taizé provided a contrasting musical sound.

None of this would have happened if the committee had abdicated its leadership, as it had done before the musician's creative suggestion. As the Center for Parish Development has shown, how we lead does not have to be reduced to a simple choice between autocracy and abdication. There is instead a wide range of leadership behaviors.[4] It is possible for leaders to provide clear direction, while at the same time to work collaboratively with the group. That is what the musician did when she boldly brought forth her discovery of the Taizé piece, but then worked with the committee to discover how best to use the music in the service.

## Confusing Gimmicks with Sound Theology and Ritual

In the story of the Pentecost service, one of the reasons that the liturgy worked so well is that the music was congruent with the Scripture and the celebration of Pentecost. The musician did not say, "I found a neat piece of music that I like and I think everyone else would like too." Instead, she presented it as expressive of the qualities of Spirit and community, which the service was supposed to embody.

A great deal of tribal warfare results from people using the power of liturgical leadership to impose forms and methods of worship that have at best a tenuous relationship to the depths and demands of faith. We remember, for example, a denominational group that met monthly and was eager to find a renewed sense of *koinonia* in its corporate prayer. Members of the group had defined the issue with great care: they wanted a deeper awareness that they were the body of Christ, joined as one by the Spirit. But this careful theological and pastoral statement of their need was reduced by the worship committee to a desire "to feel closer to one another," and the next service featured a story about "warm fuzzies."

Many members of the group were disappointed in the service because "warm fuzzies" did not have the power to help them with the strenuous challenges of their mission or to make sense out of the tragedies of their lives. Warm fuzzies were not good enough for a husband whose wife was dying from cancer or for the committee working on fair housing and another on food for the world. The planning committee needed to ask the critical question which Lawrence A. Hoffman has put in these succinct words: "Is community mere groupieness, or is it theologically resonant with the presence of God?"[5]

In this case the planning group tried to respond to the expressed need of the group but had done so without exercising critical theological judgment. The story had awakened a "warm feeling" in one of the committee members when she had read it to her small child. Then she and subsequently the committee with whom she shared the story confused that "warm feeling" with the congregation's seeking a deeper sense of their oneness in Christ.

## Finding Our Way Toward Revitalized Worship

In light of so many temptations and pitfalls it is easy to give up, to say, "What's the use?" and to glide along on "the way we have always done things"—except that sooner or later we feel the Spirit calling us toward a more vital expression of the community's faith. Therefore, we are going to name five perspectives that can encourage us in our efforts to respond to the Spirit by identifying the positive potential for liturgical renewal in the communities of faith that we serve.

## The Benefits and Liabilities of Belonging to a Tribe

If you have ever traveled to a foreign country whose language and customs were different from your own, then you know the relief of returning home, no matter how enjoyable your trip was. In your native land you know exactly how to negotiate your way with the language, with strangers and clerks. You find yourself no longer straining to be sure "you do things right" because the behaviors that you have learned from childhood and that have become second nature to you are now allowed to operate without your constant monitoring. You have more energy for being attentive to others because you are not preoccupied with the correctness of your own speech and behavior.

There is a similar pattern to the tradition in which we were raised or in which we have spent the larger part of our worshiping lives. It is our "liturgical homeland." We know its language, customs, and actions. We do not worry about "doing it wrong" because the actions have become a part of our character. Although this familiarity carries the possibility of empty repetition, it also brings the potential of intense spiritual attentiveness: familiarity means that the heart and mind are freed to give themselves entirely to focusing upon Christ, to becoming open to the Spirit without any awkward reservations about the correctness of the liturgical action.

23

We picture, for example, a Welshman who was in one of our congregations and the way he would sing any Welsh hymn. He never took the hymnal out of the rack because he knew all the tunes and words by heart. He would tilt his head slightly back and often close his eyes. His singing voice rose up with unforced power as he breathed with his whole being. The man was transformed in the act of worship by the words and music of prayer that had become a part of his spirit.

Most people who have been longtime worshipers in a tradition know certain prayers, liturgical actions, or musical selections that function in the same way as those hymns did for the Welshman. These things constitute the liturgical inheritance of the tribe that raised them. People fight hard to keep this inheritance for an excellent reason: because they experience it as the way to renew their sense of the presence of God.

Stop.

Think of what is particularly sacred to you in the act of worship.

If it is a hymn, sing it.

If it is a prayer, pray it.

If it is an action, such as going forward for communion, picture it in your mind.

If it is the structure of the entire service, go through it slowly in your memory.

If it is the worship space itself, identify the windows, symbols, arrangements, and proportions that appeal so deeply to you.

If you are reading this book with a study group or worship committee, tell the others why you chose the liturgical elements that you did. Listen to the background, associations, and history that each of these items has for the person who remembers them. Try to understand how the element functions with such power in his or her life, and why it is such a treasured part of worship.

Through this small exercise you can touch upon the depth of feeling that arises from those sacred actions and symbols that were taught us by the tribes of our origins. Tribes are necessary because people need a group that has particular customs and traditions in order to learn how to worship. So when people resist changing something in worship, it may be for deep spiritual reasons: this is the way their tribe instructed them and the way they sense God's presence.

Of course, just because a tribe has taught something in the past and just because you or I am moved by it does not make it worthy of being included in the worship of God. Sometimes tribes teach things that are unjust or that new knowledge and critical thought reveal to be distorted, and we have to ask, "Are they true for us?"[6]

We think, for example, of language that has associated darkness with evil and thus reinforced racism, or language that by its excessive male imagery for humanity and God has excluded or misrepresented women's experience. Every tribe has its own limitations and distortions, and the justice of God requires that we do not perpetuate these failings.

Consider this hymn, which is beloved not only by the Methodists with whom it originated but with many other traditions as well: "O for a Thousand Tongues to Sing." It is one of those hymns that many can sing by heart or at least with minimal attention to the page. Nevertheless, recent hymnals have suggested omitting the lines that read in the original:

> Hear him, ye deaf; his praise, ye dumb,
> your loosened tongues employ.[7]

Or they have revised the original to read:

Hear him, ye deaf; ye voiceless ones,
your loosened tongues employ.[8]

This may seem like a small matter in the telling of it, but it is disturbing if we are singing the old words from memory and all of a sudden we realize that our words are colliding with the words around us. Our state of prayer is interrupted and we wonder "who is fooling around with my beloved hymn." But our reaction may change when we consider the prejudicial treatment that is often shown the deaf, the hard of hearing, and those with speech impediments in our society. To associate the word *dumb* with these disabling conditions is to reinforce all the thoughtless jokes made in situation comedies and our general impatience with those who do not hear and speak well. And to use the word *dumb* this way in an act of prayer is to imply that the term is divinely sanctioned.

That is only one example of the need to adapt the inheritance of our liturgical tribes. However, the necessity of critical attention does not negate the value of our tribal background. The depth of feeling associated with the rituals that have shaped us tells us that there are enormous energies within the human heart, energies that can be called upon for the revitalization of worship, especially if we strive to honor all that is best in people's various traditions.

In working with seminars, workshops, and congregations over the last fourteen years, we have been impressed with how much people are willing to open themselves to the renewal of worship, *if* we begin by understanding the sources of their current practices and allegiances. Then it becomes possible to interpret the reform of worship in the light of their best memories and the highest hopes of their hearts. We are introducing reform not "to take away" from their worship, but to expand and deepen their sense of the living God.

# The Benefits and Liabilities of Pluralism and Popular Culture

We have observed in our work that it does not naturally occur to people that there are other tribal memories besides their own present in the congregation. There is often an assumption of uniformity. Perhaps such an assumption was warranted in earlier generations. We can recall when a "mixed marriage" was a Methodist wed to a Baptist! But increasing numbers of pastors tell us that they can no longer assume that new members were raised in the tradition of the congregation they are joining. Pluralism and popular culture have moved into the local church, and they have brought both liabilities and benefits.

The liability is the loss of tribal familiarity. Liturgical leaders cannot take it for granted that the congregation shares a similar background, a common body of corporate prayer and hymnody, and particular ways of doing the service. This puts profound stress on the community and the liturgical leadership:

> Since religious groups provide ultimate values that guarantee personal worth, the worship group must be cohesive enough to be able to foster a sense of the members' shared affirmation of each other as ultimately valuable from a religious perspective. Worship then does more than evoke the presence of God. It provides religious identification.[9]

The internal pluralism of the congregation and the quickly changing values and fashions of popular culture make it harder to be "cohesive" and to maintain a clear sense of "religious identification." There is a loss of the unself-conscious ease that comes with being in one's liturgical homeland. Now one must be attentive to a multiplicity of customs or at least to a significant number of people

27

who will need orientation to a different way of offering corporate prayer.

Making the issue more complex is the general state of our culture, which is permeated by individualistic and entertainment values. When our tribes were more uniform, their identity more defined and homogeneous, then the tribe itself provided a model of how to be a member of the community. I recall, for example, an older man in a congregation who mourned the passing of "When it was all clear."

"What was all clear?" I asked him.

"Baptism, confirmation, marriage, the Sunday service—we all knew when you did what and how."

Perhaps the man was idealizing the past, but his comment hints at a significant change in the life of worship. The tribes no longer make it "all clear." No longer does everyone know "when you do what and how." And a lack of clarity in the tribe leads people quite naturally to turn to other authorities in their lives, particularly the authority of the culture in which they spend their daily lives.

Since individualism and entertainment are outstanding characteristics of that culture, it is reasonable to expect that people will bring those values to bear upon their liturgical practice. There are at least two ways to interpret this encounter between the church's life and the culture, and although they seem at first glance mutually exclusive, we believe that each has something to say to the revitalization of worship.

The first interpretation sees the cultural influence as detrimental to the corporate life of the church because the values of individualism and entertainment are antithetical to the belief that we are all part of one body, not just a collection of unrelated individuals.

Furthermore, worship is not intended to be entertainment in which we observe others performing for us. Everyone present is a participant. "Derived from the

Greek, *leitourgia*, [the word 'liturgy'] was used in Hellenistic Greek of an act of public service,"[10] not public entertainment.

The authors of the widely read analysis of popular culture, entitled *Habits of the Heart,* point out that

> most [churches] define themselves as communities of personal support. A recent study suggests that what Catholics look for does not differ from the concerns of the various types of Protestants we have been discussing. When asked the direction the church should take in future years, the two things that a national sample of Catholics most asked for were "personal and accessible priests" and "warmer, more personal parishes." The salience of these needs for personal intimacy in American religious life suggests why the local church, like other voluntary communities, indeed like the contemporary family, is so fragile, requires so much energy to keep it going, and has so faint a hold on commitment when such needs are not met.[11]

We sense this fragility in almost every group with whom we work to vitalize worship. It has become a major consideration in the design of our workshops. We have discovered that in most cases we cannot assume a common understanding of a tradition's theology, history, and identity.

For example, preparing to lead a conference for a denomination whose traditions were not familiar to us, we read a textbook about their origins and the outstanding features of their worship and corporate life. We opened our time with them by sharing our understanding of their traditions, acknowledging that all we had read was one standard work on their history and identity. Many of them said out loud before the whole group, "You know more about us than we do." At the end of the workshop, when participants recounted what they had learned, the insight most frequently voiced was how helpful it was to hear something of their history and to realize the strength of their own tradition.

Even when the church members are more conversant about their historical roots, we have discovered that their knowledge tends to be removed to a level of intellectual abstraction, so that it is seldom a major factor in the participants' liturgical judgments. In such cases we cannot begin to consider the specifics of revitalizing worship until we first address issues that are fundamental to the sustained existence of any church: (1) theological integrity, (2) the place of history in forming our identity, and (3) what it means to be a member of Christ's body.

Without some common understanding of these elemental principles, attempts at reforming worship stand on shaky ground. There is the constant possibility of reducing our judgments to our immediate subjective reactions—something that will happen often enough anyway!

We remember viewing a videotape of the great hymnologist Erik Routley, laying out principles for the evaluation of a new hymnal he was about to introduce. With his usual enthusiasm and clarity, Routley made his presentation and then stood open to questions. The first question was from someone wanting to know if his favorite hymn was included. All of Routley's hard work to establish some standard other than personal favorites was ignored by this singular personal concern.

Maintaining standards of theological integrity that are greater than private preference is difficult for any age, but it has become even more challenging in an era when television "has made entertainment itself the natural format for the representation of all experience."[12] Entertainment as the "supraideology" and "metaphor for all discourse"[13] reinforces the propensity for individualistic judgments and makes it more difficult than ever to appeal to a concern for the corporate body. People who are accustomed to changing a dial whenever they are not pleased with what they are hearing and seeing probably will have little patience with a chant or hymn or prayer that is not instantly accessible and appealing, no matter how fine its theology and artistry.

The patterns that we encounter in revitalizing worship are symptomatic of a culture that honors feeling more than belief and commitment, and that lives by a philosophy of "ontological individualism, the idea that the individual is the only firm reality."[14] Thus our efforts at reform engage us with values that are at cross purposes with the goals of corporate worship. Lacking the clear tribal identity that once made it "all clear"—or at least seemed to—and working in an inhospitable culture, we may find the work of revitalizing worship overwhelming.

And yet this is only one interpretation of the situation. Michael Aune has provided an alternate and more positive reading of the encounter between the church and popular culture. He says it is "important"

> not to decry the contemporary cultural scene as simply an aberration and totally detrimental to the worship of the church. . . .
> It is unfortunate that liturgical observers and critics, because of their own unexamined assumptions and dichotomies, are not always able to see that an expectation for ritual to be powerful and fraught with sense is as much a desire and need for connection and relationship with God, with others, and with the world. These desires and needs are not always an extreme form of egotistic individualism that subverts all public and communal values in favor of purely arbitrary preferences.[15]

In other words, what we have described as liabilities also hold potential for the renewal of worship. They give evidence that there is a tremendous hunger in the soul, which is not adequately met by the church or the culture.

Of course, this hunger can take a distorted form as *Habits of the Heart* documents. But this hunger can also be a source of energy for worship renewal.

Another way of stating the matter is this: in the beginning of his *Confessions*, Augustine acknowledges that "our hearts are restless until they find their rest in thee, O Lord." Such restlessness is still alive in our own age. We can see it in the energy that people invest in clinging to the tribal customs that bring them to an awareness of God, and we can see it in other people as an unsatisfied hunger for a new definition of the self. The intensity of their restlessness suggests that there is more energy available for worship renewal than we may have realized. Revitalization does not depend entirely on those who lead worship. The energy for change is in the congregation.

We have experienced that energy firsthand when churches have commissioned us to write hymns for special occasions or to express the unique character of their community life. In each case we have visited with members of the congregation and asked them to recount what is central to their understanding of the church and its worship, what their best memories are, and what their hopes and dreams are for the congregation. If we did not put a time limit on these discussions, people would talk until the kingdom comes!

The fervor of the laypeople often amazes the pastors and musicians who sit in on our discussions. The routine of leading weekly services may have dulled their expectations so that it sometimes comes as a revelation to discover the richness of hope and yearning that people bring to worship, and especially in those from whom they least expect it.

Recently we interviewed a group of church members from a congregation that had undertaken renovations to their church that included the replacement of the beloved, but weathered, cross that crowned their steeple.

They wanted a new hymn to celebrate the restoration of their church building as a symbol of their recommitment to the ministry of Christ. It was moving to hear people talk about what the sight of the old steeple cross had meant to them over the years, not only when they came to church, but also when they passed it on their way to work or to the shopping plaza. In the world of neon lights and shopping malls, that cross had a meaning that was far greater than a casual observer would have guessed.

With the laypeople's conversation alive in my head, I (Tom) began to write the initial hymn text. When I finished, I gave it to the pastor, who passed it along to many people to get their responses. A man who was not a member of the original committee found a single stanza dissatisfying and took the time to write a well-reasoned and eloquent letter, which moved me to revise the text. He opened the letter by pointing out that he was "a biochemist and perhaps borderline Christian and was not allowed past the first tryout for college choir." This apologetic note is not uncommon among people when they are invited into any process of liturgical evaluation and planning. They think that they are not experts because they do not have the training in history, theology, and liturgics. Although that technical knowledge would be helpful to them, they contribute significantly to the discussion because they possess another kind of knowledge that is indispensable to the leaders: what the experience of worship is like for the people in the pew and how it relates to their daily ministries in the workaday world.

In the case of this particular hymn, the stanza in question read:

> Stand us straight upon our feet,
> brave enough to plant the cross

in the marketplace and street
where our faith is mocked and crossed.

Here is the critique by the self-identified "borderline Christian," the kind of person you might be tempted to conclude has little or no interest in revitalizing the church's worship:

> The stanza seems to indict "the marketplace and street where our faith is mocked and crossed," as somehow a burdensome place to overcome, whereas I feel them more the dwelling place of mugged people, including myself, in need of a neighbor. It is to meet my limitations primarily that I seek help in standing straight and being brave enough to act my faith. The marketplace and street are my partners in that search for life. They prompt me and support me. When I do act my faith, my effort is generally accepted graciously; rejections occur but never leave me feeling that my faith was mocked or crossed.

I was so moved that this man cared deeply enough to write such a thoughtful critique of the text, that I revised the stanza to read:

> Stand us straight upon our feet
> and then send us from this place
> through the market and the street
> as we bear the cross with grace.[16]

I wrote the man back and this is what I said in part:

> You describe yourself as "perhaps borderline Christian." After reading your letter and observing the care with which you interpreted your understanding of faith and its place in the world, I can only say I hope for many more borderline Christians. We need—God needs—people who are willing to be as thoughtful as you are in your letter. Nothing is more dangerous than a mindless faith. . . .

Thank you for helping to make your church's hymn a more accurate expression of faith for the time and place in which Christ Church lives and works.

We have used this example because the letters allow us to document the precise exchange. But the story is representative of scores of conversations we have had with people in the pew, people who cared profoundly about the church's corporate prayer, and who gladly joined in revitalizing worship when it was clear that the contribution of their perspective would be welcome. When we consult with churches, part of the dynamic is that we are outsiders and the task of interpreting themselves to interested strangers frees them to examine their life and to clarify meanings and yearnings that have remained unarticulated in the shadows of the heart.

We have taken what we have learned from working for and with other congregations and applied it to our own community, meeting with the worship committee three or four times in the course of a year to assess what is going on in the lives and hearts of our worshipers. We use this material not only to prepare services that address the themes and needs that emerge in our discussion, but also to stay in touch with the spiritual energy that is in the group.

We are impressed again and again with how much people care about worship and how much they are willing to open themselves to change *if* the leadership is willing to be open to them. We have found that we can count not only on the restlessness of the heart, but also on the gratitude of the heart that has been given an opportunity to express more completely the fullness of its praise and thanksgiving to God.

Thus in our experience the revitalization of worship requires a balanced critique of popular culture. We do have to be wary of the extreme individualism that can derail our efforts. The language of personal autonomy and self-fulfillment that is rampant in our society can make it difficult to comprehend the Christian vocabulary of corporate prayer, of acting together as the body of Christ. We have often encountered the "ontological individualism" that *Habits of the Heart* documents.

From our work with seminary students and pastors, we realize that "ontological individualism" is often manifest in the clergy. Once they have "a church of their own"—the language of possession is revealing here—they sometimes begin to shape their liturgical decisions entirely according to their personal taste, without consistently testing them in light of other vital standards: theology, tradition, history, pastoral need, and the particular customs of the church they serve.

The pastor's overcontrolling behavior is often not intentional. We recently worked with an ordained person in a D.Min. program who was a model pastor: a person of deep faith and integrity. He did a presentation on his tradition in which the "priesthood of all believers" is a central affirmation. This belief was reflected during the worship service by providing opportunity for the spontaneous offering of prayers by members of the congregation. Although the pastor affirmed this custom in his formal presentation, it emerged through conversation that he kept strict control over the entire service, including any prayers offered. He himself was startled by the contrast between his belief and practice, between what he avowed and what he did. He had slipped into taking more and more control.

In the case of such an excellent pastor whose general sense of self-awareness is high, we find that this move toward an overcontrolled manner of worship leadership may be the result of conflicted forces in the congregation that the pastor senses could explode. Or it may be that the pastor is aware of the culture's "ontological individualism" and is taking command in order to keep it from distorting the church's corporate life. These are understandable causes for the pastor's action, and yet this pattern of behavior is almost sure to block the energies for revitalization that are in the congregation. We are more apt to discover these energies if we balance our suspicion of popular culture with an appreciation for the hunger for God that may be disguised beneath the search to find oneself:

> We cannot forget that the desire to find a self is rooted in our inherent sociability. For good or for ill, other-regarding and societal relations are crucial to our making sense of our own lives and the world in which we live. One wonders whether contemporary interests in making worship more engaging are reflective of our contemporary psychosocial experience which both wants and fears more open, more intense, more sensitive, more loving relationships with self, others, the world, and God.[17]

A balanced critical perspective on the liabilities and benefits of our culture is a necessary prerequisite for revitalizing worship in our own age. When Israel gathered the tribes to worship at the temple, we know that they did *not* completely eschew the popular culture that was around them. Although Yahweh was presented as a jealous God before whom there were to be no others, the praise of Yahweh drew upon songs and imagery that were common to many peoples in the ancient Near East, reinterpreting them in the light of the community's faith.

A similar pattern manifested itself in the early church. Recent scholarship in "performance studies" suggests that the gospel may have been proclaimed in a number of dramatic and oratorical forms whose styles were familiar to those raised in Greek culture.[18] If the gospel was not presented as entertainment, at least it was presented in a manner that could engage people's imagination, and that would not have been possible without establishing some critical connections with the culture. The worship of the communities that gave us the Bible was vitalized by a critical relationship to culture, neither completely rejecting nor completely accepting its forms of expression.

## The Psalmist's Hope for the Gathering of the Tribes

Keeping a balanced relationship between the dynamism of popular culture and the values of the worshiping community is no easier in our day than it was when the psalmist wrote about the hill in Jerusalem where

> . . . the tribes go up,
> the tribes of the LORD . . .
> to give thanks to the name of the LORD.
> (Psalm 122:4)

As we observed at the beginning of this chapter, we do not know whether these words describe what actually took place in ancient Israel or the poet's hope for what might be: "Probably during the reigns of David and Solomon, all of the tribes did go up to Jerusalem, but how far this remained true after the division of the kingdom at Solomon's death is uncertain."[19]

Although historical certainty about the situation behind the text is not ours, the psalm reveals principles that are essential to the vital worship life of any community, including those to which we belong today. The principles sound so simple that one might think it unnecessary to name them. Yet in our experience it is the rudiments of corporate worship life that are constantly lost and that therefore need constant restatement.

The first principle is stated in verse 4: the tribes go up to Jerusalem in order "to give thanks to the name of the LORD." The praise of God draws them beyond their parochial allegiances and outshines all the excuses they might give for confining themselves to their own tribal circle. In the praise of God they find the meaning of existence, which they share with all other tribes and creatures.

Worship awakens a vision of their commonality, which in turn awakens their concern for justice, for one another, and for the wholeness of the community. We read in verse 5:

> . . . the thrones for judgment were set up,
> the thrones of the house of David.

The throne in Jerusalem would have "constituted the highest court."[20] By including this image in the poem the psalmist presents the intimate connection between worship and justice. "Liturgy and social justice may seem strange companions"[21] to our compartmentalized way of thinking, but they live side by side for the psalmist who knows that where God is truly praised, justice flows.

Worship leads to justice, and justice leads to peace:

> Pray for the peace of Jerusalem:
> "May they prosper who love you.
> Peace be within your walls,
> and security within your towers."
> For the sake of my relatives and friends
> I will say, "Peace be within you."
> For the sake of the house of the LORD our God,
> I will seek your good.
> (Psalm 122:6-9)

Having discovered their commonality through the praise of God, the tribes now pray for more than themselves. They pray for the entire community, "the peace of Jerusalem," "for the sake of the house of the LORD our God." The position of this house image at the conclusion of the psalm suggests that worship is a pilgrimage from the confines of the tribe to the just and inclusive community of God. Their home is no longer the small world of their tribal origins. Their home is "the house of the LORD our God," whose hospitality extends to every tribe.

Although the dream of praise, justice, and community was never fully realized in Israel's history, it remains an ideal for our own gathering of tribes. Praise, justice, and community are the very qualities of congregational life that we seek through the revitalization of worship. To achieve them, we need at least three things: (1) a vision to guide our efforts as worship leaders, (2) a spiritual discipline to keep that vision alive, and (3) skills and knowledge to actualize that vision.

## A Vision of Worship Leadership for Our Time

Building on the work of the Center for Parish Development,[22] we have often asked workshop participants to draw, without the use of words, an ideal vision of their church's worship, including themselves in their role as liturgical leaders. The absence of words is an important part of the exercise because it frees people from clichés that often block their thinking in fresh ways. Frequently the drawings reveal yearnings and hopes that the participants were never able to articulate until they drew them on paper.

As they begin their visions, most people give themselves with abandon to the dynamic symbols of water, bread, wine, the cross, an open Bible, the world in need, their people filled with rushing wind, and so on. But where they find themselves stumped is in figuring out how to represent their role as leaders. The problem goes deeper than one of artistic representation. When we discuss their visions it becomes clear that the role of leader is problematic because of the frequent abuse of power through which people have suffered from leaders in the past, not only in the church but also on the job and in public office. The more we talk, the more stories we hear of worship leaders who acted autocratically: pastors who imposed new liturgies without consultation, musicians who restricted selections to their singular tastes, lay leaders who threatened to leave or to dump the pastor unless things were done their way, worship committees that arbitrarily blocked or initiated change. The stories are not limited to one group, but reveal that anyone or any tribe holding a leadership role may abuse the prerogatives of the position.

The ability to envision leadership in positive ways is crucial for the worship life of a congregation. People want and need leaders who will enable them to offer their gifts to God in a communal act of praise. Churches respond positively to leaders who demonstrate a clear, theological knowledge of their tradition while remaining open to the unique character and contributions of their particular congregation.

We have found that it is helpful to explain our vision of collaborative leadership through images as well as concepts. Recent works in linguistics and theology have demonstrated that the ability to speak metaphorically about something is crucial for meaningful conversation and the development of ideas about a subject.[23]

We had occasion to give our concept of leadership imaginative expression when a friend who models such leadership was elected bishop. We wrote the following hymn, "Pastor, Lead Our Circle Dance," as a gift to celebrate the occasion, but also to help worship leaders who attend our workshops to view their role in new and creative ways:

Pastor,[24] lead our circle dance
which the Spirit has begun.
Help us hand in hand advance,
show us how to move as one.
Some demand a driving beat,
others ask to slow the pace.
Teach us how to bend and meet
our conflicted needs with grace.

From the center lead and show
steps and leaps we never tried,
then allow the dance to flow,
dancing with us side by side.
Let each dancer take a turn,
dancing in the center free
so that all can teach and learn
what our circle dance could be.

If the circle gets too tight
stop the dance and don't begin
till our open hands invite
all whom Jesus welcomes in.
For the dance of faith belongs
to the strangers in the street,
and we need their steps and songs
for the dance to be complete.

Pastor, lead our circle dance
as the Spirit leads and calls
till the circle's whole expanse
moves beyond our bounds and walls
and we dance with distant suns
dancing in the dark above,
dancing as creation runs
on the energies of love.[25]

The hymn is written to be sung by the congregation to
the leader, an acknowledgment of their need for leader-

ship and a reminder that the leader's role is to help the church function as a healthy group that moves "as one" and meets its "conflicted needs with grace."

The hymn affirms the leader's special gifts: "From the center lead and show/steps and leaps we never tried," but this is balanced by an equal commitment to drawing on the gifts of the entire group: "Let each dancer take a turn."

However, the task of leadership does not end with caring for the church's internal concerns. Whenever the church is perfecting its "dance" there is always the danger of forgetting the world. Consumed with building up group life, we gradually find that our efforts at revitalizing worship have led us to

> make our most serious mistake. We romanticize community. We think that community should provide the intimacy of the family. We criticize large parishes. We complain of liturgical assemblies made up of strangers. Perhaps we even point to the Lord's Last Supper, a dinner shared by intimates, as our model for celebration. We forget that all was not sweetness and light in the upper room and that another old tradition sees the feeding of the multitudes as the institution of the Eucharist. We forget that the major parable Jesus told about community concerned the relationship of two strangers. We forget the Emmaus story, where two disciples find the Risen Christ not in their friendship but when they reach out to a stranger.[26]

To develop the church's dance while keeping the circle open "to the strangers in the street" is more than any of us can do merely by ourselves. This is why the hymn ends with the congregation reminding the leader to follow the Spirit so that the total process of revitalization leads the church into a deeper union with the praise that fills all of God's creation: "and we dance with distant suns/dancing in the dark above,/dancing as creation runs/on the energies of love." The musical setting for the hymn text may be found at the end of this book.

## Spiritual Discipline to Keep Our Vision Alive

The rhapsodic conclusion of the hymn reminds us of our need to keep alert to the Spirit in our own lives. This might seem self-evident, but we have discovered that is not at all the case. Because liturgical leaders are continually planning and leading services, it easily becomes for them "just my job." The sense of mystery and wonder, the awe of handling holy things grows dull through familiarity and routine.

Leaders need a regular discipline to maintain their own alertness and receptivity to the Spirit. Such discipline can take many forms: daily Bible reading, singing or reciting hymns, meditation upon simple events and objects, periods of silence, a regular time of personal prayer, and so on. Our purpose is not to prescribe any one type of discipline. Its manner and shape will vary according to an individual's temperament and background. But what we stress is its importance to the sustenance of a leader's vision and to the impact upon the character of the leader. Congregations intuit whether or not their liturgical leaders are in fact people of prayer, and over time that has a profound impact upon the effectiveness of the services at which they preside.

In recent years we have become quite concerned that clergy and church musicians do not themselves regularly have an opportunity to worship without the burden of preparation and leadership of the service. We used to be of the opinion that this was not necessary, that their offering of their gifts as leaders was an act of prayer adequate to the feeding of their own hearts and minds. There is some truth to this view: musicians and pastors tell many stories of how they received grace and power through the act of offering the gift of their liturgical leadership.

But at the same time we have become aware that no matter how prayerfully they lead the service, their role requires them to be concerned with details in a way that never allows them to become "lost in wonder, love and praise." Following worship at the workshops we lead, many participants tell us: "It was wonderful to give myself completely to the prayers, the hymns, the reading and preaching, and the receiving of the sacrament with no need to worry about taking care of how it is going."

Reflecting on the frequency of this comment, we have come to see the great wisdom that some groups of clergy have shown in regularly gathering for worship among themselves. One of their number takes responsibility for the service so that the others can worship with a suspension of critical consciousness that they cannot afford in the congregations they serve.

We have also observed with sadness that meetings of many denominational groups have reduced their time of worship in order to fit in more business. This represents a profound dislocation of values and practices essential to Christian community. No amount of organizational work will revitalize the church if the flame of worship is dying out. As an ordained person reported over the lunch table at one of our conferences: "After we reduced the time of worship and extended our business meeting, we ended up getting less business done. All that the change accomplished was to give us more time to go over the same arguments we had already heard." Many heads nodded in agreement, and in the sad voices of those who told similar stories we detected the loss of visionary power that results from the atrophy of worship.

## Skills and Knowledge to Actualize the Vision

Although we stress the necessity of personal and corporate spiritual discipline, we also realize the importance of analytical skills and knowledge in the revitalization of worship. An exclusive reliance on religious and theological language can be a way of avoiding the well-reasoned judgments that need to be made about what is wrong in our worship and how to improve it.

Unfortunately, many church members, including the clergy who may have had minimal or no training in liturgy during their seminary years, lack terms for adequately expressing their experience of worship. So they are reduced to saying things such as: "It wasn't spiritual enough." "It was very moving." "I liked it." "It spoke to me." "I didn't like it." "The music seemed wrong." "I enjoyed it."

Sometimes, the inability to articulate their feeling stems from associations that reach back to childhood, responses that are in the bone and blood. Nevertheless, we have found that when we offer terms and concepts that help people organize their experience, their behavior changes. Instead of simply emoting, they begin to give an account of their responses that makes conversation with others possible.

We find a parallel in what we are describing in medical advances that have helped people describe their pain more precisely. Research shows it is not enough simply to talk about the intensity of pain. "It hurts bad, Doctor." Instead, it is useful to provide patients with a series of related words—for example, flickering, quivering, pulsing, throbbing, beating—which enable the sufferer to "bestow visibility on the characteristics of pain."[27]

Liturgical analysis requires terms and concepts that can "bestow visibility" not only on the characteristics of what pains us about our current practice, but also on our hopes for the revitalization of worship. As people learn to bestow visibility on the deep realities that are in their hearts and minds, they can better understand their own responses to worship as well as the responses of others. They can then join in the pilgrimage of the psalmist who said, "I was glad when they said to me,/'Let us go to the house of the LORD!'" (Psalm 122:1).

In the chapters that follow we develop theories and terms that bestow visibility on the great prayerful yearnings of our churches so that all the tribes can gather "to give thanks to the name of the LORD."

# CHAPTER

# Worship and Music
## *Hearing Again the Harmony of the Spheres*

Many of our most precious videotapes are not on VHS. They are in our memories, and we play them on the screen in our minds as we recall the churches where we have prayed and sung God's praise.

We see a piano with some missing ivories and hear a flattened barroom sound. But someone is playing with a secure beat and a conviction that draws the whole congregation into song. We picture the choir room and people running in for the last minute warm-up. We view a magnificent organ and hear the sound of tin and wood pipes suggesting the elusive mystery of the Spirit singing in the soul. We observe the faces of particular singers and instrumentalists whose eyes are intently focused on their musical leader, searching for the nod or the motion of the hand that will direct the precise entrance, the graceful phrase, or the fiery crescendo. We replay all these scenes, and our hearts feel again that lift of the Spirit that came as the church filled with music.

But there are also other tapes: people standing with their arms folded while others are singing hymns; a governing board with angry faces discussing the place of the arts in budgetary priorities for the church; someone with stern eyes telling the music director that the changes to a favorite hymn are offensive; a pastor and church musician exchanging stressful last minute instructions before they begin to lead the service.

## Musical Education: A Cultural Challenge

From the music of the spheres to discord and dissonance—that is a range of experience familiar to nearly every congregation. The discrepancy between our best memories of music that lifted our hearts to God and the conflict occasioned by musical differences is one of the most stubborn and baffling phenomena of worship leadership.

How are we to understand this discrepancy?

Are we merely at the mercy of each of our individual musical tastes, as diverse and unconnected as the various tribes who blared their different music from radios in the park? Will we dismiss the possibility of a solution by blaming our conflict on what we deem music's inexplicable and unruly powers? This has been a common strategy throughout the centuries:

> The temptation to regard the effect of music on a hearer as Irrational, and the working of those effects as Mystery, is a deeply rooted one. The history of the abandonment of the imagination of Western man [and woman] to that temptation is long and complex.[1]

There are ways of resisting this temptation, ways to bring order and understanding to the entanglements of worship and church music.

First we need to realize that a significant part of our problem arises not merely from forces within the church, but also from a society that is experiencing the consequences of "the almost total defaulting of our educational environment and the resultant stranglehold in which the commercial interests have been able to hold the fine arts for decades."[2]

What are the first items to be cut when the school budget is under stress?

Music and art!

The result is that most people lack any basis for making informed judgments about the character of the church's musical ministry. The primary values that influence them are those implanted by "commercial interests," and this means that instant accessibility and gratification of personal taste usurp the more enduring qualities of truth, tradition, community identity, and spiritual depth.

It is instructive, for example, to compare people's musical illiteracy with the sophisticated knowledge that most of them have of their favorite sport. They can discuss the nuances of a game and can make keen judgments about how an athlete is or is not performing. If someone else joins their conversation, they can quickly tell if the person has the requisite knowledge to talk about the sport. Much of this knowledge comes from having participated in the sport through their growing up years, and then assiduously reading the sports pages and watching the most gifted athletes perform.

In no way do we dismiss the satisfactions and challenges of becoming knowledgeable about a sport. Our point is simply to illustrate how far most people are from any similar knowledge of music, which is as complex and nuanced a human endeavor as any sport. We do not ask someone to coach who has no familiarity with the game, yet worship committees and pastors are frequently making musical judgments without any exposure to the elemental principles of music, including the seemingly simple act of listening. W. A. Mathieu observes:

> As a culture we have forgotten how to listen to music. Music has become devalued currency, ubiquitous and banal. I'm glad that music is everywhere. I'm not glad that the purpose of its being everywhere is to sell you some-

thing, like records, for instance, or more food at the store. *In less civilized cultures music is everywhere because all the people make it. Singing, dancing, clapping, drumming, and playing instruments are ways of being together, or of being alone.* But most of what we hear in our culture is recorded. Music has become a specialty given over to professionals. Even though it seems like music is closer to us because it is everywhere, it is actually farther away.[3]

I (Carol) recently had a personal experience of the truth of Mathieu's observation. Two of my teenaged daughters and I were on a long road trip when they suggested, half in jest, that we make the time pass faster by singing with one another. Remembering all the times our family used to sing on long trips when I was growing up, I asked enthusiastically, "What shall we sing?"

It turned out that all my daughters were able to remember were a few silly songs from childhood such as "the ants go marching two by two, hurrah, hurrah!" and some jingles from television commercials. The rock music they listen to was not practical for singing because its effects depend upon an incessant beat and loud accompaniment. Its melody was not strong enough to stand alone.

Making music as a way of "being together" is no longer possible for most people because, as Mathieu says, "most of what we hear in our culture is recorded." With the advent of mass broadcasting and recording, people came to associate music with passive listening or even more frequently as background noise for other activities, and so they have forgotten that the most joyful experience of music is making it.

I believe my daughters' request, "Let's sing together," despite their jesting tone, represented some dim but genuine awareness of what satisfaction it would bring to blend our voices in song. They had a glimmering of the pleasure of singing together, but a performance-dominated culture provides no support for the desire to join in mutual music making.

The only place where people continue to sing together on a regular basis is in church, and the very sight and sound of

> a crowd of people singing aloud in unison is a cause for wonder even for people who are accustomed to it. To see row upon row of people standing, not before an audience in a concert hall, but directing their chorus simply toward the front of the church, where stands a pulpit with a Bible on it, a large table, and one or two persons dressed in long white robes, is surely an experience like no other to be ordinarily encountered from day to day. What brings these people here? Who are they singing for, and why? What is going on?[4]

It is indeed "a cause for wonder" as well as thanksgiving that congregations are still praising God in song. But their gathering together is often marked by severe strains over what music they will sing and play. The lack of musical education in the culture only serves to aggravate these conflicts since it leaves people without the background they need to express and understand their differences.

## The Theological Importance of Music in the Church

Since the performance culture of the mass media fails to nurture the rudiments of confident music making, the church will have to educate its members. Given all the demands on the resources of the church, this may at first seem like an item far down on the list of ecclesiastical priorities. But we believe it should be near the top. If you doubt this, just think of what happens when there is an explosion over music in a church: people retreat to their own tribes, and the energies for mission get siphoned into

51

overcoming internal alienation and hurt. The realities of group life require that we give high attention to the musical expression of a congregation's worship. People who sing together stay together.

But there are even deeper reasons for considering the church's music to be essential to the church's life and work. The vitality of the church depends upon the mutual interaction of music and theology:

> Music and theology are interrelated and interdependent. The Bible is concerned with practical theology, the understanding and explanation of the interaction between God and man [and woman], and also with practical music, the accompaniment to that interaction. Theology prevents music from becoming an end in itself by pointing man to its origins—in the doxology of creation. Music prevents theology from becoming a purely intellectual matter by moving the heart of man to consider its ultimate purpose—the doxology of the new creation.[5]

Note how music and theology are held to be complemental to each other, each keeping the other from slipping into its own distortions. "Theology prevents music from becoming an end in itself by pointing man to its origins." Most of us can think of times when music has altogether displaced theology in the church and we have come away feeling we had been in a concert hall.

We recall a church that had a long tradition of presenting a special musical service during the Christmas season. For many years the service included readings from the Bible, prayers, carols, and hymns by the congregation, and several extended and challenging pieces by the choir; sometimes even a major work with instrumentalists, the kind of thing that would be too big in scale for a Sunday morning anthem, but which gave a sense of wonder to this annual occasion. The choir and soloists used to sing in their choir robes and the conductor directed from his seat on the organ.

But over the years the original format began to erode and shift until there were no readings from the Bible, no congregational song, and no prayers—only a few words of welcome from the pastor. The conductor now hired someone to play the organ while he stood on a podium in a tuxedo, and although the choir wore their usual robes, the soloists were in evening dress. The entire event had changed from a musical service of worship to a concert, and there was an uneasiness in the congregation about the whole thing. They still loved the choir and the beautiful music and they did not want them to stop their efforts. They simply did not want the music to displace the theology, the pointing to God's love in the incarnation of Jesus Christ, which had been so apparent when there were Bible readings, prayers, and congregational carols.

As one woman said, "When we had those things they made the music more beautiful." The woman had a refined musical sensibility, and she was not suggesting that religious talk substitute for music, but rather that the language of prayer did exactly what Robin Leaver claims: it "prevents music from becoming an end in itself" by pointing us to our origins.

On the other hand, music is equally corrective to the distortions of ecclesiastical verbosity: "Music prevents theology from becoming a purely intellectual matter" by moving the human heart to consider its ultimate purpose.

I (Tom) recall a dramatic instance in which theology completely displaced music to the starvation of a congregation's spirit. It was one of a number of services commemorating various figures from the Protestant Reformation of the sixteenth and seventeenth centuries. On this particular occasion there was a reenactment of a liturgy of Ulrich Zwingli (1484–1531), and true to the reformer's practice, there was no singing or playing of music during the entire service. At first, the effect was rather striking. Accustomed to excellent organ music and full-voiced congregational song, the people found refreshment in the leanness and quietude of the service.

But after the sermon, great fidgeting set in. The preacher had drawn on Zwingli's writings to illumine what the Bible means today. As people talked after the service, they all agreed it was excellent preaching, but they felt cheated by the absence of music. The sermon had lit a fire in their hearts and they thirsted to sing. One person said: "I considered getting up and begging: 'PLEASE let us sing a hymn.'" The interest in historical verisimilitude had evaporated as their hearts ached to sing in response to hearing God's word preached with such power.

This story is an extreme case, but in the extreme we see magnified what happens when faith becomes too talky and loses its musical voice. No less a reformer than Martin Luther knew this, and that is why he insisted that musical knowledge was a necessary element of sound theology and affirmed its place in the life of faith.[6]

Next to the Word of God, music deserves the highest praise. She is a mistress and governess of those human emotions—to pass over the animals—which as masters govern men or more often overwhelm them. No greater commendation than this can be found—at least not by us. For whether you wish to comfort the sad, to terrify the happy, to encourage the despairing, to humble the proud, to calm the passionate, or to appease those full of hate— and who could number all these masters of the human heart, namely, the emotions, inclinations, and affections that impel men to evil or good?—what more effective means than music could you find? The Holy Ghost himself honors her as an instrument for his proper work when in his Holy Scriptures he asserts that through her his gifts were instilled in the prophets, namely, the inclination to all virtues, as can be seen in Elisha [II Kings 3:15]. On the other hand, she serves to cast out Satan, the instigator of all sins, as is shown in Saul, the king of Israel [I Samuel 16:23].[7]

If we take seriously that music is a gift of God, then it will be apparent that music requires the same attentive stewardship as the use of any other gift from God. Unfortunately, the ubiquity of music and the ease with which we can turn the knob to a radio or disc player have conditioned us to be as profligate in the use of music as we are with the gifts of the earth. Stores, banks, waiting rooms, offices, shopping malls, elevators, telephones put on hold, supermarkets, restaurants, airplanes, car radios, neighborhood stereos, and portable tape decks pour a ceaseless stream of music into the air until God's gift is reduced to background noise and robbed of its deeper spiritual resonances.

W. A. Mathieu is convinced that it requires disciplined effort to be fully engaged by the beauty and power of music. It is not something that automatically happens to us, anymore than we automatically know how to pray or to understand the Bible. Mathieu interweaves his reflections on music with simple practical exercises that people with no musical training can practice. These exercises are designed to help us regain our capacity to respond to the riches of music. Here for example is one of the opening exercises:

> Listen to the sounds you are hearing now. Then close your eyes and listen, and open them again. Try to hear the same way in both cases. Notice how the eyes are with the ears.[8]

This appears to be so simple a matter that one would almost wonder why one should bother with it.
But try it.
Try it alone.
Try it together as a worship committee.

People often make judgments about music without really having heard it at all. The initial notes have been filtered through their established patterns of reception and are either immediately welcomed or rejected. What Mathieu's exercises provide is a way of opening ourselves to the spiritual dimension of sound:

> In the act of hearing, you experience a part of the creation that made you, something that has been alive from the very beginning, something you almost remember. Sometimes when you listen to music you could swear you actually do remember. The music lets you witness the original spark. Each tone becomes a metaphor for the moment of your origin. "You never lost it," the music says, "no matter how long it's been gone. It's here now, here now."[9]

Music is more than ornament or something that enlivens our worship. It is a gift that helps us remember the source of our creation. Making and listening to music can be, therefore, a form of spiritual discipline, an act of prayer that makes us aware of our relationship to God:

> How often, making music, we have found
> A new dimension in the world of sound,
> As worship moved us to a more profound
> Alleluia![10]

"A more profound Alleluia" is the goal of music as a spiritual discipline. When we are making decisions about music for worship we are doing far more than choosing this or that piece. We are building (or blocking!) ways for the congregation to offer "a more profound Alleluia," a more complete and faithful expression of praise to the One who has made us and redeemed us and sustains us every moment of our lives. This requires that we who are entrusted to make such decisions practice music as a spiritual discipline ourselves.

# Three Ways to Recover Music as Prayer

Here are three things that a worship committee could do that would help them recover a sense of music as prayer and as a gift of God that demands the same faithful stewardship.

1. Use selected chapters and exercises from W. A. Mathieu's *The Listening Book*. Because the chapters are brief (sometimes only a page) and the exercises are simple, they could be used during a period of prayer and meditation at the beginning of a worship committee meeting.

2. Include the singing of hymns and other forms of congregational song at every meeting of the worship committee. Most denominations have brought out new hymnals in recent years, and this means that there is a large body of fresh material that could help revitalize a congregation. But just having it between the covers of a book will not make the riches available to the congregation. The worship committee will need to read and sing its way through the hymnal from beginning to end, making their own index, thinking creatively about when and how the new music should be presented.

3. Along with singing through the hymnal, work with a handbook on congregational song that will help musicians and nonmusicians alike to gain some basic principles and ways of talking about what they sing. For example, two modestly priced paperbacks that are concise and written in language for the nonspecialist are Alice Parker's *Melodious Accord: Good Singing in Church* and James Rawlings Sydnor's *Hymns and Their Uses*.[11]

The goal of all three of these activities is to regain our capacity to listen and respond to music at greater depths, to recover our sense of music as prayer. This is not an extraneous activity, something to do if you have some spare time as a committee. Rather it is central to leading a congregation toward "a more profound Alleluia."

Because the disciplined use of music requires time and energy you may be tempted to abandon it, and to justify your action by claiming that the church has more important things to do, especially in reaching out to a world in desperate need. This distinction, however, between the church's music and mission is entirely fallacious. It is one that breaks down the minute we look at the place of music in empowering people to witness to their faith and to stand for what is good and right.

For example, Sally Belfrage, remembering the civil rights movement in Mississippi in 1964, recalls how those seeking justice found strength, not simply in the rousing speeches of its leaders but in the group solidarity that came as they sang together:

> There were more songs, and finally we stood, everyone, crossed arms, clasped hands, and sang "We Shall Overcome." Ending every meeting of more than half a dozen with it, we sang out all fatigue and fear, each connected by this bond of hands to each other, communicating an infinite love and sadness. A few voices tried to harmonize, but in the end the one true tune welled up on them and overcame. It was not the song for harmony; it meant too much to change its shape for effect. All the verses were sung, and if there had been more to prolong it, it would have been prolonged, no matter how late, how tired they were. Finally the tune was hummed alone while someone spoke a prayer, and the verse struck up again, "We shall overcome," with all the voice, emotion, hope, and strength that each contained. Together they were an army.[12]

Music and mission, like music and theology, are complemental. A church that neglects music will eventually find its powers for outreach and justice eroding.

## Religious Ambivalence About Music

Despite music's power to inspire the church for mission, there is a long history of suspicion about this gift from God. It is important to consider that history, since all of us are shaped by attitudes and values from the past even when we are not aware of their influence upon us.

The ambivalence toward music emerged in ancient times. James Anderson Winn has traced how music and poetry began together, how they shared a unity in their rhythmic affinities and the songful inflections of the human voice. The Greeks even "used a single word, *mousike,* to describe dance, melody, poetry, and elementary education."[13]

But over time this unity was replaced by growing tensions between those who used words and those who used music as their primary medium of expression. Initially the conflict was known in trying to set strophic texts to a repeated melody in which "a melodic or harmonic effect designed to imitate or express some particular word in the first stanza usually falls on a less appropriate word in subsequent stanzas."[14]

To put it another way: the verbal text was considered to be the most crucial element in the song, and the standard of musical judgment was how well the tune went with the lyrics. Music all by itself was suspect:

There was, by and large, a suspicious attitude toward textless, purely instrumental music on the part of Greek thinkers. . . . One of the fundamental reasons for the disapproval of the music of the *aulos* or oboe involved the fact that the performer thereon cannot sing while he is playing, as in the case of the lyre, *kithara,* or other stringed instrument.[15]

59

The problem moved from the classical world into the practice of Western liturgical music, which initially featured "a similar closeness of text and tone."[16] The marriage began to break up with the development of polyphony, music in which many melodies are sounding simultaneously so that "the importance of the *meaning* of the text was greatly reduced."[17]

That the "meaning" might be lost in music, that the clearly reasoned word might be usurped by the sensuousness of pure sound, is a fear that haunted Augustine and fueled his ambivalence about the place of music in the liturgy:

> I see that all our spiritual affections, in keeping with their diversity, have corresponding modes of voice and song and are stirred up by a kind of secret propriety. But this sensual pleasure, to which the soul must not be delivered so as to be weakened, often leads me astray, when sense does not accompany reason in such wise as to follow patiently after it, but, having won admittance for reason's sake, even tries to run ahead and lead reason on. Thus in such things I unconsciously sin, but later I am conscious of it.
>
> Sometimes I avoid this very error in an intemperate fashion, and I err by an excess of severity. Then I strongly desire that all the melodies and sweet chants with which David's psalter is accompanied should be banished from my ears and from the Church itself. . . .
>
> But again, when I recall the tears I poured out on hearing the Church's songs in those first days of my recovered faith, and how even now I am not moved by the singing but by the things sung, when they are sung by clear voices and fitting modulation, I again recognize the great utility of this institution.
>
> *Thus do I waver between the danger of sensual pleasure and wholesome experience.*[18]

The fear that music will entice the heart and that the heart's fervor will disengage the mind's critical functions is the basis of Johannes Ruber's novel, *Bach and the Heavenly Choir*, in which a fictional Pope Gregory wants to canonize J. S. Bach and meets with opposition from cardinals who are

> convinced that the Holy Father's reasoning was thoroughly dangerous. What Gregory was trying to do was to penetrate into a world where even the bravest would lose his reason. . . .
>
> That the simple, saintly Francis of Assisi was a saint was not beyond the understanding of the believer, but that God should reside in works of art was not a thing that could be taken for granted; for often art was wretched, a thing of the devil. Art had always evaded man's attempts to define it, and many who had taken it upon themselves to try had come to grief on its real secrets, as the ancients realized. Poets and musicians had fallen into madness, or had ended by committing suicide.[19]

Gregory answers his opposition by pointing out that "'countless people have gone to their homes after hearing [Bach's] music withdrawn into themselves, and there have thought of God. Their thoughts have amounted to prayer. And how many have not been moved first by him to live in the way of the Lord?'"[20]

Ruber's book is a work of fiction, but his insights about the powers of music and the fears those powers evoke are rooted in the division that frequently exists between the disciplines of music and theology.

At the beginning of this century Sidney Lanier remembered "when the most flourishing church of our town regarded with intense horror a proposition to buy an organ, considering it an insidious project of the devil to undermine religion."[21] And in one of our workshops, a participant told the humorous story of the ancestors of his own congregation: "The Session had ruled that no musical instrument should be 'brought through the doors of the Church.' So the youth of the parish brought one (an organ) through a window."[22]

All of these stories are the acting out of an attitude that has surfaced again and again. A scholar of the history of the attacks upon music and musicians describes how vehement the opposition sometimes became:

> The very height of venom in attacking music-makers was probably attained long before the middle of the sixteenth century, if not by zealous patristic writers condemning secular music in order to belabor the flute-girls of the theaters, then certainly by medieval churchmen like the twelfth-century Aelred, Abbot of Rievaulx, Yorkshire, who in a famous passage in his *Speculum Charitatis* attacked the liturgical music of his own day. . . . From the medieval moralist's condemnation of minstrels to the complex series of struggles for status by professional musicians in the sixteenth century, a constant stream of attack aimed at the practitioners themselves often eclipsed any more sophisticated arguments against music pure and simple.[23]

In our many years of leading workshops in worship renewal we have had firsthand experience of the surprise that music can evoke. We recall a particular Sunday service that we had designed in collaboration with members of a congregation. They had invited us to lead a daylong conference on the Saturday preceding the service. During that Saturday session we had introduced one of the hauntingly beautiful refrains from the ecumenical community of Taizé: "Jesus, remember me, when you come into your kingdom," words of one of the thieves crucified next to Jesus (Luke 23:42).

The congregation sings the phrase again and again to a rich chordal accompaniment and a descant on a flute or other melody instrument. Because they keep repeating the refrain it is quickly established in the congregation's memory, so that they can put down their books and give themselves entirely to the act of praying through song while the instruments support and lead them. The piece has enjoyed ecumenical acceptance and has found a place in a spectrum of recent new hymnals.[24] To understand our story fully, you might take time to try the music if it is available to you.

We had introduced the music on Saturday, and people had found it to be deeply prayerful. They had sensed their need of the Savior through the repetition of the thief's prayer and they had felt Christ's reassurance and peace flowing through the musical accompaniment. This was not the *"vain* repetition of prayer" that Scripture warns against, but rather a repetition that opened the doors of our hearts wider and wider to Christ.

When we sang the music in the service the next day, there was a palpable sense of wonder among the congregation. Afterward, we evaluated the service. Many people were thankful for the way "Jesus, Remember Me" had deepened their sense of the Spirit. But one man, a participant in the worship planning process on Saturday, had not realized how strongly the music would affect him on Sunday. During our evaluation, he turned the full glare of his eyes upon me (Carol) as the musician and said with resentment in his voice: "You knew what you were doing."

Further discussion revealed that he was a man who, by reason of temperament and profession, was always in control of himself and his surroundings. But singing this tender music with a congregation of people who were visibly moved had drawn him into giving expression to his own deep feeling. The experience reminded him of forces he usually kept under tight rein. Other members of the group pointed out that the piece had been offered in the middle of the service, allowing the more traditional music and prayers that followed to reestablish the congregation's customary sense of order. The security of what was well known brought the people to an emotionally less vulnerable state as they prepared to leave the church to go forth into the world.[25]

The man was reasonable enough to grant that what they said was true, but the tone of his accusation, "You knew what you were doing," carried the fury of one attacked by surprise. He had agreed the day before that he liked the piece for its power, but when its power moved him beyond his usual limits of control, he turned against the music and the musician.

We believe that the ambivalence toward music is a manifestation of the ambivalence toward God, for music is frequently held to be an expression of the divine. When Virginia Woolf writes the following words she is confessing what many have felt in Western history:

> Certainly I should be inclined to ascribe some such divine origin to musicians at any rate, and it is probably some suspicion of this kind that drives us to persecute them as we do . . . to many, I believe, [the musician] is the most dangerous of the whole tribe of artists. . . . It is because music incites within us something that is wild and inhuman like itself—a spirit that we would willingly stamp out and forget—that we are distrustful of musicians and loath to put ourselves under their power.[26]

We want to give ourselves to the music, yet we fear what will happen if we do. We want to give ourselves to God, yet we fear what will happen if we do. These are more than parallel statements. The first is an expression of the second.

The Bible depicts both our hunger for God—"My soul thirsts for the Lord more than the deer for the stream"—and our fear of God—"Where shall I go to escape from your spirit?" But we are not usually as direct about our negative feelings for God as the biblical writers. The piety of most of our churches presumes that we will always thirst for God, always desire God. As a result, our prayers, unlike the Bible, do not normally give expression to our ambivalence about God.

Nevertheless, our ambivalence remains. We still need to express our mixed desire to surrender to God, yet to stay in a position of control. Since music is associated with the divine, it often becomes the arena in which we manifest our ambivalence toward God. Our responses to music bear the weight of our spiritual struggle. This helps to account for the passion that usually fills people's voices when they talk about music that has disturbed them in worship. Through music they are dealing with their relationship with God, the center of faith, the reason they have come to church in the first place.

Given the nature and history of the ambivalence toward music, it is no wonder that people often despair of straightening out the struggle in their local congregation. And yet there are at least two excellent reasons for believing the church can effectively address the problems that flow from our ambivalence toward music: the first is spiritual and the second is technical.

The spiritual reason is to be found in the nature of creation. There is an impulse for adoration in all living things, and there is a need in human beings to give expression to that vital force through music. Such mysteries are better expressed through the evocative language of poetry than prose, so here is how we would put it in verse:

> The song and prayer of birds
> is melody alone.
> Their hymns employ no words.
> Their praise is purely tone.
>
> Their song is prayer enough.
> Love hears what sound conveys,
> and love does not rebuff
> a creature's wordless praise.

And so we trust that prayer
does not depend on words
to reach the source of care
who understands the birds.[27]

We can confidently approach the complexities of music in church because we know that underneath their ambivalence human beings share with other creatures the irrepressible impulse of song. This spiritual conviction is more than a pious afterthought. It is one of the beliefs that empowers us to gain and use the technical knowledge required for revitalizing worship.

## Clarifying the Function of Music in Worship

Our knowledge of the history of ambivalence toward music can help to free us from unexamined assumptions and fears. We can begin to clarify the function of music in worship and the role of the church musician.

We have seen that music may bear deeper meanings than we initially suspected, including the burden of our ambivalence to God. In addition to this theological weight, music often carries with it the force of personal memory. The poet Anne Sexton provides a vivid description of how this works in our consciousness. She says, "music swims back to me." Think of all the times that music swims back to you, a tune rising out of your past and bringing back a distant memory:

Music pours over the sense
and in a funny way
music sees more than I.
I mean it remembers better.[28]

That better memory includes the feeling of the event in your heart and soul, the emotions of joy or grief which the music first expressed, or which surrounded the event at which the music was heard. These are released anew as the "music swims back" to you.

It is often this personal memory and its associated feelings that animate the way people defend favorite hymns or the music that was sung at their weddings or at a family member's funeral. If, for example, a new hymnal provides a different musical setting for a familiar text that is more singable or more appropriately expressive of the words, some people in the congregation will express anger that appears to be out of proportion to the change that has been made. The upset is not simply about the words and the music, it is about the memory and the feeling that are kept alive when the familiar music "swims back" to the listener.

I (Tom) think, for example, of "What a Friend We Have in Jesus." As a small boy, I used to visit my mother's family in the rural South. Sunday was always a full day of church, and as a youngster raised in a more reserved Presbyterian congregation in the North, I was fascinated by the energy of the singing I heard in the small Methodist parish where my uncle took me. What I remember above all things was the way the people sang "What a Friend We Have in Jesus." It was their church's signature song. If I hear just the first two measures of that hymn or if the "music swims back to me" when I am daydreaming, I am instantly back in that church standing next to my uncle, whom I loved to visit. I have memories of his opening the King James Bible from which he read every morning before we had breakfast. I have memories of his taking me fishing and later in the day sitting on his lap while he drove the tractor, sometimes absentmindedly whistling, "What a Friend We Have in Jesus."

Notice here the enormous amount of mental association which the hymn awakens but which belongs to me as an individual. The personal memory is so completely fused with the memory of the hymn that there is no way I can hear the music without awakening the feeling of those childhood days, even when the particulars elude me.

To associate a hymn about Jesus as friend with an uncle who was an adult friend helped to shape a positive experience of faith early in my childhood. Yet for all the values that we can celebrate in this story, there are also dangers in it. I may unreasonably expect that the church will continually nurture my personal memories. I may displace the corporate function of congregational song with my private meaning, forgetting that Christian worship is in part an act of group memory. The church gathers to recall what God has done, and the hymns of the past serve to keep us interwoven with the web of memory that forms our tradition and understanding as a church.

It is important to stress that this is the church's memory, not simply a collection of individual remembrances. We come together to recall what we as a corporate body remember, and therefore our principle of musical judgment and selection cannot be reduced to the set of memories of any one individual.

Of course, the church cares for individuals, and of course, we hope that a significant portion of the church's musical expression will engage the deep personal memories of the congregation. But these are not in themselves adequate standards for understanding the function of music in worship.

To lift up a broader corporate understanding of music's liturgical purpose is not to be unfeeling toward individuals. Because of our privatistic culture we tend to think that the way to care for people is always to respond to their immediate feelings. But, in fact, we can often be more helpful by providing resources for renewal which their feelings have blocked from view.

I (Tom) recall a day when I went to worship and was obsessed with a problem that I had turned around and

around in my mind. At every turn it had the same unsolv-
able appearance. Then we sang the opening hymn:

> Immortal, invisible, God only wise,
>     in light inaccessible hid from our eyes,
>     most blessed, most glorious, the Ancient of Days,
>     almighty, victorious, thy great name we praise.[29]

The melodic outline of the major triads that open the
hymn combined with those great words of wonder,
"Immortal, invisible," snapped something loose in my soul.
I was no longer circling around and around the same problem. I was swept into a state of prayer from which I later
returned with fresh energy to address the situation that had
worn me out before I left it behind to attend worship. The
church had provided me with pastoral care *not* by asking
me what I was feeling or what I wanted but by directing me
to the chief end of all human existence: the praise of God.

This is not to say that we never address direct personal
concerns through our worship and our musical selection.
But it is to affirm that these decisions must always be
guided by the psalmist's principles, which we explored in
chapter 1:

> . . . the tribes go up,
>     the tribes of the LORD . . .
>     to give thanks to the name of the LORD.
>     (Psalm 122:4)

Music in the church has a trans-tribal purpose: it is to
help the tribes gather as one "to give thanks to the name
of the LORD." This means that the tribes cannot afford to
act like the tribes in the city park where they turned up
their radios and tape players to drown out the others, so
that there was nothing but cacophony. If the church repli-
cates that kind of musical imperialism in worship, then its

proclamation of reconciliation and community will carry no authority.

In bringing clarity to the function of music in worship, we have found the following statement of the Roman Catholic Bishops' Committee on the Liturgy illuminating for churches regardless of their denominational identity:

> *The function of music is ministerial*; it must serve and never dominate. Music should assist the assembled believers to express and share the gift of faith that is within them and to nourish and strengthen their interior commitment of faith. It should heighten the texts so that they speak more fully and more effectively. The quality of joy and enthusiasm which music adds to community worship cannot be gained in any other way. It imparts a sense of unity to the congregation and sets the appropriate tone for a particular celebration.[30]

Because the function of music in worship is "ministerial," the principles of selection and judgment are more complex than if its function were purely to entertain or to provide a refined artistic experience. Ministerial does not imply that there is to be no concern about the aesthetic quality of what is chosen. But it does require a much broader understanding of what would be appropriate for a congregation, given the wide diversities of background and need that are present when people gather to pray.

We recall a woman who once asked us about the services in which we participate daily at our seminary: "What style of music do you use as a community, folk or traditional or gospel?" She assumed that any worshiping community would have a fixed style of music, and that a congregation could not mix various types of music that are supposedly incompatible.

The woman's assumption is a common one among many people who grew up before the 1960s when the congregational song of most denominations possessed a voice that was distinctively their own. But that situation has now radically changed, as reflected in most of the major new hymnals that have appeared in the last few years. Thus, when we were writing down the story about the man who was powerfully moved by the music from Taizé, we discovered that the piece in question, "Jesus, Remember Me," was in the first four hymnals we took off the shelf. The music has a 1981 copyright, and there were few selections of equal simplicity in the denominational hymnals of earlier generations.

This one example is symptomatic of a major shift in congregational song toward a wider diversity of styles and traditions. The shift includes an intentional effort to reflect the ethnic pluralism of the church and to make local congregations more aware of the worldwide Christian community by including music that is indigenous to a variety of cultures. Many of the most recent English language hymnals include stanzas in other languages as a way of heightening the global consciousness of the congregation.

The shift toward a greater pluralism of musical idioms makes it possible for the music to serve a "ministerial" function to a wider range of persons. A more inclusive repertoire of congregational song makes clear that the church is serious about justice and reconciliation.

The editor of a recent new denominational hymnal tells how a Native American wept when she discovered that one of her people's favorite hymns was to be included. The woman said, "I never believed that I would live to see the day when you would count the songs of my people worthy of your singing." When we recall how music often bears the meaning of our relationship to God and how it is associated with our deepest memories, then we can glimpse into the depth of the woman's reaction. The fact that the denomination was willing to sing her people's song was an affirmation of their theology and their history, a symbolic action that spoke with great power.

Hospitality toward another people's song is not something that comes automatically. Although we often say, "Music is the international language," it does not always work out that way, especially when the musical idiom is radically different from the music we have grown up with. This was brought home to us at an international conference on hymnody. People gathered with the best of intentions to sing and learn one another's music, and in most cases their goal was splendidly realized. But we recall an occasion where one group tried to interpret itself to another. They made a sensitive presentation that opened not with their music, but with the music of the other group! They played it and said that they understood how precious this was to their listeners. Now they wanted to share what was equally precious out of their ancient traditions of worship. But after they did so one person rose to ask, "Why did we have to listen to that noise?"

Although an extreme reaction is always a possibility when people try to understand each other across cultural boundaries, we cannot permit the fear of this happening to keep music from serving a wide range of people. We have discovered that it is possible to break through the presumption of the incompatibility of contrasting musical traditions, and that when it is done with care it often provides an opening for the Spirit to work in powerful ways among the congregation.

We think of a special Lenten service that was being planned by an ecumenical and interracial seminary class. The choir was going to offer Bach's Cantata #78, "Jesus, Thou My Wearied Spirit," which is based on a chorale of the same name. The group had worked carefully with me (Carol) in preparation for conducting the instrumentalists and choir. The most perplexing question for the planners was what the final hymn would be. Many of them wanted to sing the gospel hymn "Alas! and Did My Savior Bleed" because the words of the hymn and the cantata were similar in their focus on the agony of Calvary.

But one person objected strenuously. Even though he loved "Alas! and Did My Savior Bleed" as a hymn of his own tradition, he said it did not "fit" with the music of Johann Sebastian Bach. I pointed out that in word and music it was a quality example of its own genre, which, while not the same as the Bach music, had its own integrity. The hymn would contribute to people's understanding of the theme of the service through its own unique expression of the message, which it shared with the cantata. There was a long and hard debate about the hymn, but in the end the one who protested its use agreed to go along with the group as "an experiment."

At the conclusion of the service he came up to me and said with tears in his eyes, "You were right." Further discussion with the man revealed that the beauty of the instruments and voices in the Bach cantata, and the fervent prayers of the people had drawn him into wanting to sing the hymn. The rhythmic vitality of its musical setting, HUDSON, especially in the refrain, transfigures the cross into a sign of victory. And this was exactly the right complement to the weeping music of the cantata. In the act of worship the contrasting musical styles became a source not of conflict, but of completion.

This story illustrates the importance of acknowledging the many voices with which music speaks and sings to us. It also tells of the value to the worshiping community of the musician, who is prepared to interpret music's potential for theological expression and reconciliation. Such a musician is able to minister as a change agent in the congregation, rather than become a warrior for one tribe or another.

The story of the cantata reminds us that the selection and presentation of hymns, anthems, psalms, and instrumental music requires the same thoughtful attention as the preparation of the sermon and prayers, for music, like preaching, is a means of ministry to, with, and among members of the congregation. To sustain that ministry requires not only clarity about the function of music in worship, but also clarity about the role of the musician.

## Clarifying the Role of the Church Musician

For many years it has been popular in our culture to discredit the importance of roles and to favor the expression of our true selves. Although we all need occasions when we are not burdened by the roles that we fill day by day, roles are, in fact, an inescapable part of being a member of the human community. The careful definition of a role can be liberating because it clarifies what our responsibilities are. Most of us have experienced embarrassing situations in which we were not quite sure what to do, and we have explained afterward, "I was not sure what my role was."

Sometimes, however, we get caught because the definition of our role no longer fits our situation. If we hold the same position for several years we often find ourselves no longer doing the things we were hired to do and taking up duties we never imagined. We may negotiate these changes gracefully for a while, but there often comes a point of conflict when the organization or our boss or our own sense of purpose compels us to take stock and to redefine our role. That is exactly what has happened with the role of church musician. Enormous forces and movements in church and society have transformed the role from what it once was.

To get a feeling for the change in role let us compare a description of church music that was published in 1956 with two advertisements for church musicians that appeared in the *American Organist* magazine, October 1989.

Here is Leo Sowerby writing thirty-five years ago:

> The worshipper must not expect that church music will "sound like"—that is, be of the same type or style as—secular music, for it should be quite evident that profane and worldly influences should be eliminated. However, it is not demanding too much to expect that it shall be of the same standard of excellence as that of music heard in the concert hall.[31]

Obviously these are the words of a man who has never had to deal with a worship committee or a choir member who has just come home from a weekend retreat that featured songs for personal spiritual renewal or a pastor who is hopelessly prone to supporting the musical opinion of the last parishioners who stridently expressed it. The fifties were times when ministers and musicians knew their roles and their place in the proper order of churchly things. There was little question about the "right" music for each denomination.

Now consider these more recent items from the "positions available" column of the *American Organist*:

> Part-time organist-pianist. One Sunday service; weekly choir rehearsal; periodic special services. Other special areas of responsibility: children's choirs, high school music, assisting in evening service at piano or synthesizer, arranging music for instrumental or vocal ensembles, teaching music in church elementary school.

> Full-time minister of music for 2,300 member congregation. Applicant should be committed to the Christian faith and the place of sacred music in worship. Responsible for coordinating total music ministry, including direction of chancel choir, youth choirs and bell choirs. Minimum of five years' experience and master's degree preferred.[32]

The difference in the role of the church musician between Sowerby's era and our own is that keyboard and choral skills are only two of the *many* skills required nowadays by the job. The role requires far more than furnishing prelude, postlude, three hymns, and a choir anthem as in former times. Instead, musicians find themselves thrust into the role of musical leader, having to negotiate the complexities of the ministerial function of music in worship. When music took to the streets in the freedom marches of the sixties, many recognized for the first time its capacity to bring a sense of unity among those singing, particularly when the songs expressed beliefs that were strongly held in common by the singers. An awareness of the transforming power of "the folk" singing and of music's ability to move and to teach people was renewed among us then, and church members now seem unlikely to return to the passivity of earlier eras.

The central point in comparing Sowerby's words and our present situation is this: before earthshaking forces began to transform the church during the sixties, there was an acknowledged right way to fill the role of church musician. But now there is no longer a standard role definition, no longer a generic right way, but rather, *many* right ways. The role now requires that musicians seek to determine what is appropriate for the particular occasion in which a particular congregation gathers to worship God. This is a decision that involves the balance of a large number of interrelated and sometimes conflicting needs, including:

- the church's tradition
- the ever-expanding repertoire of congregational song
- what resources are available
- current history
- acoustical environment
- liturgical developments within the denomination

- the state of the relationship with the pastor and worship committee
- the pastoral needs of the community
- and the kind of musical leadership that is available among the people.

The complexity of the role reflects the complexity of the function of music in the life of the contemporary church. Musicians, pastors, and worship committees need to work collaboratively to define the role that will be most effective for their congregation's life. What is appropriate in one setting may not be in another. Pastors know this from their experience of moving to serve a different congregation. The sermon or approach to teaching that worked in the last parish may not work in the new location. And the same is true for music. This is why it is crucial that there be some mutual understanding of the musician's role among the clergy, musician, and congregation.

Such understanding needs to consider not only the congregational and cultural forces that we have been examining, but also an appreciation for the unique gift and calling of the musician. Just as the musician needs to be sensitive to the dynamics of congregational life, so also the congregation needs to be sensitive to the creative vision of the musician. The church has not always been good at this. We think, for example, of the shoddy treatment that was accorded a pastoral musician whose harmonies were attacked by an unsympathetic member of the ruling church board. The name of the musician: J. S. Bach.

Not every musician is a Bach, and not every musical idea is appropriate for a particular church, but there must be breathing room for the musician and encouragement to try some of the riskier, more challenging pieces that provide a new opening for the wind of the Spirit. An overcontrolling congregation is as deadly as an overcontrolling musician or pastor. The issue is respect for the God-given talent and faith that lead each of us to our ministries. At their best, congregations realize that they must honor the integrity of the preacher's vision or they will only hear what is comfortable and never receive God's disturbing word. Likewise, if they fail to allow the musician adequate opportunity to lead them toward a richer musical diet, they will quench the Spirit that moves through the artist's imagination.

We need the new life and insight that imagination can supply:

> Perhaps never before in our planetary history have imagination and creativity been so critical. It is the process of imagining the whole symphony which gives the composer courage to take pen in hand and write the first note. It is the imagining of the same symphony which encourages the cello player to learn the part. It will be the imagining of a global civilization which will call us out of complacency and our anthropocentric (human-centered) world view to begin to act creatively to build a future which values all life.[33]

Most church musicians are not writing a symphony for Sunday, but they are involved in a musical activity that can be just as imaginative in its own way, if the congregation will allow them room to exercise their creative gifts. In our experience, this cannot happen unless the pastor understands the importance of music and takes initiative to maintain a sound working relationship with the musician.

## Clarifying the Relationship Between Musician and Pastor

The division that exists between music and theology, especially in the training of people for these different callings, is often acted out in the relationship between musician and pastor. We have encountered this division in churches, seminaries, and denominational groups whose goal is liturgical renewal. People tend to interpret the schism simply as an issue of conflict between the pastor and the musician. However, we are convinced that to focus all our attention on interpersonal dynamics is to cast too much of the burden on individuals, when the problem lies in our failure to approach music and theology as mutually enriching disciplines.

Pastor and musician both need to possess an elemental knowledge of the assumptions, skills, and vocabulary of each other's respective disciplines. Without this knowledge communication becomes difficult, and even the best intentioned efforts at collaborative ministry become strained.

Over the years we have led a number of workshops in which we perform a skit that portrays an excellent working relationship between musician and pastor. The small drama shows them evaluating a recent service and making future plans for the music and worship of their church. The play is based on what we know to be possible between pastor and musician when they possess a common vision of their task and a sufficient understanding of each other's vocabulary and perspective. Every time we do the skit—no matter what the denomination or the particular background of the participants—there is nervous laughter as the pastor understands what the musician says and the musician shows an appreciation for the pastor's particular concerns. In the discussion that follows the play, the reason for the laughter emerges: the skepticism of most participants that there could actually be this kind of working relationship between pastor and musician.

When we ask people to name what went right in the drama and why, some can. But the skepticism of other people is so deep that they ignore why anything worked well and begin to project their past bitter experiences—as either musician or pastor—upon the characters of the play. One person even asked that we replay the last scene and have the pastor in the skit give a preemptory "No" to the musician, "Just so we'll see what she does."

When there is this much alienation and a lack of common vocabulary and vision, a church's worship life pays a terrible price. The finest theology and the highest quality of musical performance cannot in themselves redeem the situation. The theologically trained person tends to favor the sophisticated use of language. The training of musicians is primarily focused on aural, sonic qualities.

The contrast in perspectives that such training brings about has been especially evident to us as a poet and composer of new hymns. Whenever we are introducing our work before it is published, the ministers are content to see the words and the congregational melody line while the musicians crowd around the keyboard to see the accompaniment. The pastors are primarily interested in the texts and what they *mean* while the musicians are eager to know about the *sound* of the piece and how the accompaniments are structured.

This is not to say that ministers are not interested in music or the musicians in language, but it is to point out that their fundamental orientations are different. By virtue of their gifts and training they are attuned to different aspects of reality, while their positions of liturgical leadership in the church require that they work as colleagues.

Although we know of some excellent professional collaboration between pastors and musicians, that has been more the exception than the rule in our experience. Every time we offer a workshop we discover again the gulf that exists between most worship leaders and musicians. We think, for example, of the blank stares that often greet us from clergy when we suggest that the choice and introduction of hymns need to be done in consultation with their musician, examining the musical values of a setting as well as the theological and poetic appropriateness of the words.

Or we think of the hostile stories told by workshop participants: a minister explains how his choir director refuses to be responsible for making sure that all the lights are out and that the building is locked up after rehearsals. The musician does not want to "demean" the dignity of his professional identity as an artist. The pastor describes the situation with barely contained rage in his voice, explaining how he does not feel "demeaned" when he is required to look after the details of closing up for the night.

This last story touches off the anger of a second pastor, whose wife, a church musician in a parish other than his own, has been undervalued and inadequately paid throughout her professional life. He sees the other musician's refusal to close the doors and shut off the lights as a cry against the injustice and lack of recognition that many musicians experience in the church.

These stories are representative of dozens that we have listened to. After every workshop, participants ask what to do about the conflict in their churches between pastors and musicians. Clergy who have had excellent instruction in pastoral care often lack any sense of how to converse in a professional way with one of the single most important colleagues in their ministry: the church musician.

The story works in reverse as well: the musician, inexperienced in discussing theology and often feeling powerless, is fearful of beginning a conversation with the pastor about the way music functions in the liturgy. Sometimes musicians view their contribution entirely from the perspective of performance without considering how it fits with the liturgical and pastoral needs of the congregation. This approach becomes even more problematic if the musician's tastes are confined to a particular style, thus failing to realize

> that quality, creativity, and high craftsmanship can and do exist in all forms and categories of music. So can and do

their opposites: mediocrity and absence of quality. *No form of musical expression is either inherently blessed with quality or intrinsically devoid of it.*[34]

Musicians lacking this awareness may subject a congregation to their own predilections while the pluralistic character of the church is crying out for a wider range of musical expression to reflect the full spectrum of the community's prayer.

For example, we were meeting with a group of musicians to plan the liturgies for a retreat that their congregation was sponsoring. We indicated that we wanted a good cross section of their community's music, including some hymnal that is central to their tradition. They held up a small collection of folk songs, written within the last twenty years, most of them featuring anemic words and predictable chord patterns, and said: "This is our tradition." Their constricted musical practice had led them to cut off their congregation from centuries of excellent music, which comprised a large part of their church's tradition. This is more than aesthetic travesty. This represents the corrosion of Christian identity and our need to keep alive the memory of the cloud of witnesses, whose prayers and music have preceded us and whose witness has made possible our present faith.[35]

We are not categorically opposed to folk music in worship. We gladly use such pieces when they are the appropriate expression of the community's praise, but the church needs musical leaders who will help the community maintain its historically grounded identity as well. Without this, the riches of the church's liturgical experience will never be effectively realized in the local congregation.

We are convinced that the situation is not beyond redemption. We believe that the first is to expand our thinking about theology and music in two major ways: (1) by developing a more positive appreciation for the nonverbal dimensions of the Word (*logos*), and (2) by understanding music as a pastoral art.

## The Word That Is More Than Words

The training that most pastors have received for ministry is distorted by relying almost exclusively on discursive thought. Ironically such an education impoverishes the capacity of language by confining us to levels of cognitive meaning that do not give adequate recognition to the evocative power of speech. This is a weakness that contemporary homiletics is beginning to redress in its concern for the oral nature of effective preaching, those poetic qualities that T. S. Eliot associated with the

> auditory imagination . . . the feeling for syllable and rhythm, penetrating far below the conscious levels of thought and feeling, invigorating every word; sinking to the most primitive and forgotten, returning to the origin and bringing something back, seeking the beginning and the end.[36]

If we understand this "auditory imagination" to be complemental to our powers of reason, then those of us whose dominant medium of communication is discursive language may come to see how the arts are a necessary ingredient in theological education. Without them our exploration of the *logos* is distorted because its focus is too constricted.

To contrast the ministry of the Word of God and the ministry of music represents a human dichotomy of what in truth is one divine reality. We hear the Word of God spoken in the sermon, but that same Word may come to us in another form through the music.

I (Tom) think here of an individual who went through a grave period of doubt at one point in his life. He was no longer able to hear the word through Scripture and sermon, but he kept coming to services for the music alone. He would always arrive early enough for the prelude and sit through the end of the postlude, because as he later put it, "They were the sermons I was able to hear then." Every time the organist began to play, that human soul was hanging in the balance. Eventually doubt dispersed, and the man could receive the word once again through human speech, but he would have given up long before that if the word had not come to him through music during his time of crisis.

## Music as a Pastoral Art

What is true for pastors is true for church musicians: it is not an adequate preparation for their ministries to be trained only within the limits of their discipline. As we have already seen, the role of musicians has shifted over the last three decades so that they are constantly having to deal with many matters that are not purely musical in nature. The church now requires of its musicians not only excellent performance skills, but also sensitivity to its theology, tradition, and pastoral need, and an ability to work with the increasing diversity that marks our communities. We cannot assume these qualities to be innately present in musicians. They represent basic ministerial arts which, like all other arts, require talent, instruction, and practice.

The concept of "pastoral music" is helpful in identifying the essential elements for educating such leadership. The term was coined and developed by Virgil Funk, who established the National Association of Pastoral Musicians. At the time, the Roman Catholic Church was feeling the cumulative impact of the reforms that flowed from the Second Vatican Council. Reclaiming the practice of the ancient church in which the liturgy is the prayer of the whole assembly and not only that of the priests has had enormous musical consequences. Previously, most church musicians had a more modest role of playing the organ and conducting the choir. But now they were faced with a great number of new tasks: choosing congregational music from the flood of new material being published; introducing vernacular hymns and service music to congregations; dealing with the pressures from various constituencies to use one particular style of music; encouraging people to sing who were not accustomed to congregational song and many of whom were baffled by the changes in their church; dealing with the resistance that was inevitably encountered in trying new things; working with clergy, who themselves had never received training for the kind of musical/liturgical coordination that was now needed; coping with the divisions of the church into different congregations according to musical style.

As one musician put the matter to Virgil Funk, "We need something that focuses on the changes that are taking place in Catholic liturgy, not just techniques for organists."[37]

This was more than a Roman Catholic need. The same basic issues were alive in Protestant churches as well. Although most Protestant denominations already had strong traditions of congregational hymnody, their music and worship inevitably felt the impact of several major movements: the hymn explosion that started in Great Britain in the 1960s; the influence of street music—much of it associated with the church's social witness; the proliferation of musical resources, including the new material of the Roman Catholics, which in an ecumenical age was welcomed by many Protestants; the Pentecostal movement among members of established churches, who were eager to have present in their Sunday worship the music that they associated with experiences of spiritual rebirth; the loosening of denominational identities as local churches found their congregations more pluralistic and their new members asking to sing hymns from the traditions that raised them; the tensions set off by the revision of liturgical language; and the conflicts of producing new hymnals.

Church musicians whose training had focused on the "dynamic level, touch, attack, duration" of notes played on a keyboard suddenly found themselves needing the skills of negotiation, interpretation, education, and pastoral care as these were informed by theology and liturgics. They found themselves having to ask:

Why am I choosing this hymn and not that one?

How will I not simply pit this person's prejudices against my own?

How can I help the pastor to see that the music is not simply filler here, that it brings completion to the prayer?

How can I say no to the group that wants to sing this piece that is bad theology and bad music?

Even many people who had formal education in sacred music, who knew the major corpus of Western religious music, and who were skilled organists and choral conductors were not ready for the complexity of the situation as it developed over the last thirty years.

The resulting lack of clarity about the professional identity of church musicians along with inadequate ecclesiastical recognition of their ministries and poor remuneration have led to a sharp decline in people acquiring the necessary skills. For example, the Buffalo Chapter of the American Guild of Organists has published a pamphlet, "Organists . . . An Endangered Species,"[38] and a study by the Association of Anglican Musicians points up the advanced age of A.G.O. members and concludes: "Apparently young people are not entering church music. . . . Apparently nothing is planned to attract people to the leadership of church music."[39]

If this situation is not addressed through an educational program that equips people with the wide range of musical and pastoral skills they require and that grants adequate recognition to the importance of their ministry, then commercial concerns will take control of the community's prayer. This has already begun to happen with the advent of prerecorded accompaniments for choirs and congregations. The very concept is antithetical to most fundamental understandings of prayer as openness to the sovereign Spirit of God.

Good congregational singing is a breathing reality filled with nuances of inflection and communal sensitivity to the other voices about us. In the mystery of our blended song we open ourselves to the way the Spirit moves among us as a particular people of God: the note that one congregation stretches out, another congregation moves through in one beat. These are sonic manifestations of how particular people pray. To replace these with one standard prerecorded accompaniment does not allow for the living reality of how we are bound by our communal sense of prayer. If we are going to prerecord music, why not prerecord the whole service: the prayers, the preaching, the sacrament? Turn the nave into a cinema and let people watch the service and have all their praying and singing done for them.

All of this may sound farfetched, but the advertisements for canned music are already circulating in our churches. Let us be clear about this: we are talking about the soul of our faith—the living praise of God. We can never let machines take over the very reason for which we were created. Yet that might happen if the church does not adequately prepare leaders in pastoral music.

Note the two words *pastoral* and *music*. Pastoral music education takes both of them seriously. Musical excellence is essential to the successful practice of the discipline. And it is helpful to musician and nonmusician alike to list some of the basic skills, most of which take years of practice and experience to develop:
- accurate technique at the keyboard and an ear tuned to the mixture of timbres

- a critical sense of what distinguishes a tune of enduring value from one that is simply immediately appealing
- an ear for discerning when a voice or an instrument is sharp or flat
- an ability to set a steady and reliable tempo
- knowing how to highlight the melody or the inner voices of a piece
- acquaintance with the great spectrum of Western music and the salient characteristics of its different styles
- an even closer knowledge of the musical traditions of the denomination being served
- the ability to assess what one can reasonably expect from a particular group of voices and how to draw forth the best music that is in them
- sensitivity to the subleties of accompanying the congregation's and the choir's music, knowing when to give in to their ritards and when to lead them strongly on, lest they drag things to a standstill.

This is just a partial list but it gives some idea of how artistically demanding it is to be a competent church musician. However, the demands do not stop at the end of the musical staff. The adjective in the phrase "pastoral music" is as important as the noun. We have already pointed out in our analysis of the church musician's changing role that it is not adequate to be only a performing artist. Many other kinds of knowledge and skill are required:

- a basic grasp of theology, Scripture, and history and how these have shaped worship in the church
- an understanding of the communal forces and tensions that are present in congregations and how these often converge around the worship service and its music
- a perspective on how music serves to awaken the prayer and ministry of people, even those who are not gifted musically but who still have a need to sing their Creator's praise
- the ability to handle conflict

- a facility with words so that the reasons for musical decisions can be explained in ways that nonmusicians can understand
- an attitude of flexibility that balances one's sense of artistic standards with the realities of a congregation's limits and needs
- a sense of what it means to be a colleague with the pastor so that the planning and leadership of worship can be a collaborative effort
- the spiritual grace to communicate through one's leadership how music is a gift from and a witness to the One who is the source of all that is true and beautiful

## Practical Goals and How to Meet Them

These lists may at first seem overwhelming. "We're just a little church and we can never attain these standards." But actually to name what is required is less overwhelming than to waste our energies in constant misunderstanding because our judgments are based on vague and imprecisely defined needs. These lists can help musicians, pastors, and worship committees assess the strengths of the ministry of music and name areas they would like to improve. If pastoral music receives adequate support from people with authority in the church, then the musical/liturgical life of congregations will become a source of renewing power for the church and its mission.

Having identified goals, there are many ways to reach them. Here are three:

1. Set aside money each year for the continuing education of your pastoral musician. There are many excellent, very reasonably priced workshops that are offered by groups such as the American Guild of Organists, The Hymn Society in the United States and Canada, and by denominational associations of musicians. In addition to

teaching about the skills we have named, these conferences often provide inspiring services of worship where musicians and pastors give strength to each other and build up their courage for the hard work they face at home.

A regular budget item could also be used to sponsor a scholarship to give a young person piano or organ lessons as a way of training future leadership or meeting your present needs more adequately.

2. If you are a very small church and you can afford only a minimal sum, join with other churches in your geographical area or make a proposal to your local denominational body—diocese, conference, district, association, presbytery—to hire a music consultant who can work with several church musicians on a regular basis as well as be available to provide advice on specific needs.

We know of one denominational group in our area that did this, and was able to strengthen the keyboard skills of several musicians from small rural churches. Their improved playing resulted in increased vitality for their worship services.

3. If it is within your financial means and you have someone who has already received professional musical training at the undergraduate level, look into helping that person enter a master's level program in pastoral music. You may be able to negotiate for a commitment of so many years service in return for your help defraying the educational costs.

This list is intended just to get you started thinking. Whatever you do, do not prematurely decide you can do nothing. Our experience is that money will often be forthcoming when people hear and experience the positive benefits of strengthening their musical leadership.

Furthermore, it is often possible to combine musical goals with other goals for the church's ministry. For example, we often fret about how to motivate people to come to church and forget that God has planted in them a need to make music, to give expression to the deepest yearnings in their hearts to praise the One who made them. We think of congregations who have practiced evangelism by welcoming young people to play in church the instruments they have learned in school, congregations that have built intergenerational understanding through bell choirs whose members ranged from age ten to over seventy, congregations who drew downtown business people to midweek prayer that featured special instrumental music, and congregations who have organized educational programs around the study and singing of hymns.

Notice in all of these examples that the expenditure of funds is for more than "just music." The music is a vehicle of outreach, care, and education. Its function is ministerial. By supporting music, the congregation is not indulging in a luxury, but supporting the ministry of the church to its members and the world.

## Why It Is Worth the Effort

Attention to pastoral music as an art of ministry is essential to the renewal of worship. That process of renewal has been well served by the work of scholars, theologians, and the committees that have been providing our churches with exciting new hymnals and worship books. But the implications and meaning of their work for the present age can never be realized in local congregations unless equally careful thought is given to the art of pastoral music.

Recently, I (Carol) attended a service of worship that exemplified the value of the discipline of church music as a pastoral art. A friend's teenaged son died unexpectedly. The funeral was held in a church that I do not regularly attend, but which practices the ideals of church music that we have presented in this chapter. The clergy and the pastoral musician fill their roles with exemplary dedication and competence.

91

On this tragic occasion the pastor read about King David's response to the news of his son's death: "The king was deeply moved, and went up to the chamber over the gate, and wept; and as he went, he said, 'O my son Absalom, my son, my son Absalom! Would I had died instead of you, O Absalom, my son, my son!'" (2 Samuel 18:33).

The choice of Scripture was exactly right, for what could we do but weep that one so young and so filled with promise should die. And yet perfect as the words were, both for their expressive content and for their symbolic weight as words of Scripture, they were not adequate in themselves. Even read with feeling and dignity by the pastor, they evaporated too soon from the air. We needed some way of letting the words distill themselves into our act of mourning.

An anthem based on the scriptural words was offered, an anthem that rose up with weeping dissonances and gave aural manifestation to the weeping in our hearts. The words were so few, but the music helped us to cry. The music extended and repeated the words. The music expressed our moaning although it was more than moaning. As its dissonance moved toward the resolution at the end, there was a catharsis of grief. We were not singing, but in listening to this perfectly chosen piece we found the music releasing what was beyond our speaking.

At the time I was not thinking analytically about the experience; only upon later reflection did it become clear what that moment of powerful pastoral care required. To deliver this kind of spiritual support at a moment of desperate human need does not happen by chance. It happens because over time musician, pastor, and worship committee have been willing to invest the energy and resources that music as a pastoral art requires.

If anyone asked us why it is worth the effort we would tell them this story and other stories like it: stories of tears, stories of joy, stories of faith, awakened by the Spirit moving through the ministerial art of pastoral music.

# CHAPTER 3

# Maps and Images
## *Giving Shape to the Yearnings of the Heart*

C. S. Lewis has compared the difference between theology and faith to the difference between maps and the sea coast. You can study a map and trace the shape of the shore. But the sound of the crashing waves, the wetness on your feet, the beauty of the foam flowing back down the strand, and the smell of the salt air are not available from the map. You have to go to the shore and walk the beach and hear the rolling thunder of the breakers and plunge beneath the waves to experience the ocean.

Theology and faith are similar. Theology is helpful in understanding the shape of Christian belief as it has been passed on to us through the centuries. But to feel the power of faith and the lift of prayer in our hearts we have to surrender ourselves to the act of believing; we have to give ourselves to the song and prayer of the church. Merely talking about it will not suffice.

Nevertheless, maps are essential, especially if you are trying to avoid dangerous shoals and cliffs or to locate a strand of beach that is known for its excellent surf. Sometimes when we leave the beach we mark on the map where we have visited, the places that are not as good, where we want to return, and where we would like to visit in the future.

We need "maps" to understand our experience of worship. Without a map it is difficult to locate the exact reasons why a particular service was such an appropriate expression of our praise or why a prayer or a hymn or a ritual action was an ineffective means of worship. The maps cannot substitute for the actual experience of worship, but they provide a way to understand where we have traveled as a congregation and where we want to go in the future.

We now present five different liturgical maps, and illustrations to show how they are useful in the analysis of worship. Study the character of your congregation's services by using the maps to review what is going well and what needs to be strengthened when you gather to praise God. Do not feel that you must be defensive if upon analysis you see many things you need to reform and strengthen. The problems that the maps reveal are not simply the result of individual decisions or of people deliberately misusing the role of leader. Often people have made changes in worship with the best intentions, but with insufficient thought about the consequences of the changes they instituted. The maps can help you find your way to a revitalized worship life.

## Map One: Structure and Anti-structure

The first map we use represents our modification of the work of Urban Holmes III. Reflecting the insights of social anthropology, he suggested that there are two poles or primary categories of experience that are *both* essential to the vital spiritual life of a community.[1]

One of these poles represents the secure elements of our worship, which communicate assurance, order, clear definition, dependability, things under control. For example, the order of our usual Sunday liturgy or a creed or covenant that we regularly recite or a well-known hymn that marches solidly forward and that is so familiar we hardly need to look at the page to sing it—these elements are the "structure," the ordering and defining characteristics of our worship.

The other pole represents the more elusive, mysterious, and uncontrolled aspects of worship where there is a richness of meaning and a depth of feeling that exhausts the capacity of verbal description. For example, the celebration of a sacrament or music that awakens such a sense of the holiness of God that we find all our inner voices falling still in wonder. These elements draw us toward the "anti-structure," reminding us that no matter how satisfying the "structure" is to our desire for order and clarity, the One whom we worship is far greater than any of our established conventions.

To get a feeling for the difference between structure and anti-structure, imagine yourself taking a stranger to your worship service. Assume that the person has never attended Christian worship and is completely ignorant about the faith. Handed a bulletin by the usher, the stranger asks about this piece of paper listing various prayers and numbers. With a little bit of instruction you can explain how to use the bulletin to find the hymns and prayers. The bulletin is a structural element, it has a precisely defined purpose.

But now the stranger points to the front of the church and asks why a giant letter "t" is hanging in the center of the front wall where everyone can see it. You explain that it is not the letter "t," but the cross.

"What is the cross? What does it mean?" asks the stranger.

To answer this question will take a lot more explanation than the bulletin! The church has been working for two thousand years to understand the meaning of the cross, and the work is still going on. You will be able to tell the stranger some of the things that the cross means, but any statement will strike you as incomplete because the cross is a symbol and symbols are part of the anti-structure, suggesting dimensions of divine reality that our words can never exhaust. You can say "#288" in the bulletin means to turn to the hymn assigned to that number in the hymnal. But you cannot offer one simple sentence that will tell all about the cross.

According to this theory *both* structure and anti-structure are essential to the vital worship of the congregation. If we came to church and no one had any idea of what the order was, we could not worship together as a congregation.

On the other hand, if the order were perfectly clear, but we just went through the motions, never feeling engaged by the elusive mystery of the living Spirit of God, then we would never say, as did the disciples returning from Emmaus, "Did not our hearts burn within us?"

Excellent worship is continually interweaving structure and anti-structure. Holmes uses a technical word to describe this interweaving process. The word is *liminal*, which means "on the boundary."

This is what the map would look like if we were to chart the worship life of a vital congregation:[2]

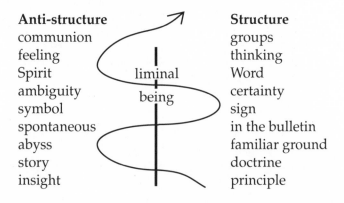

| Anti-structure | | Structure |
|---|---|---|
| communion | | groups |
| feeling | | thinking |
| Spirit | liminal | Word |
| ambiguity | being | certainty |
| symbol | | sign |
| spontaneous | | in the bulletin |
| abyss | | familiar ground |
| story | | doctrine |
| insight | | principle |

Vital worship is on the boundary between structure and anti-structure. It draws upon the orderly elements that give us a solid feeling of being related to history and tradition. But at the same time it takes us into the unexplored territory of anti-structure, which renews our astonishment at the love of God and opens us to fresh winds of the Spirit.

Here is a story in which we use this map to understand what went wrong with the worship of a particular congregation and how they found their way to more vital worship.

The church had a dedicated new pastor who had come through a difficult period in life, drawing strength and comfort from a kind of religious song that involved flowing melodies supported by soothing progressions of chords. The congregation could pick up the melody after hearing it only once. The words were as simple as the tunes. The music and words consistently expressed an understanding of God as life's dependable source of comfort.

The church members were initially glad when the new pastor introduced this music because it broke through what had become an overly constricted worship life. The new music awakened a sense of anti-structure that their strictly ordered worship had failed to provide, allowing them to get free of the printed page and to sing directly from the heart.

However, the new pastor soon began choosing exclusively this style of congregational song. Some members of the congregation remarked that it was difficult to walk out of the service after the last hymn because they felt they were still "swimming" in the music. Many members of the congregation began to resist because the assurance of their solid traditional hymns was no longer sufficiently present in the service. Things came to an impasse until the pastor, finally realizing what had happened, began listening to the people and restored their old hymns while employing the new style of music more judiciously.

The map of structure and anti-structure clarifies what happened in this story. The new style of music had provided a sense of liberation to the pastor who was working to get free of an overburdened past. But the level of the pastor's personal need for anti-structure was not the same as the congregation's. Although the people in the pew appreciated the flowing power that was conveyed by the music, they also required the connection with tradition and the stability of their familiar hymnody.

We have shared this story with people at scores of workshops, and it inevitably has drawn forth nods of recognition and yet more examples from the participants. Some of their stories are about too much structure, while others are about too much anti-structure. In either case the worship of the church suffers.

The map points us to the necessity of balance in our liturgical life. The maintenance of such balance is difficult for at least two reasons. First, there is always the possibility that we, like the pastor we have just described, will confuse our internal need with the need of the larger group. Second, the same elements of worship sometimes function in different ways for different members of the congregation; what is structure for some is anti-structure for others. We have become aware of this through our workshops when we have sung various forms of congregational songs and asked people to categorize them as tending more toward the structural or anti-structural pole of worship.

Certain pieces appear to awaken almost universal agreement about their nature. For example, if we play and sing "O God, Our Help in Ages Past" to its well-known setting, ST. ANNE, people inevitably say it is "structural," while their response to the flowing refrains of Taizé, such as "Jesus, Remember Me," which we discussed in the last chapter, draws a unanimous judgment of "anti-structure." But many songs and hymns draw contradicting judgments depending upon the background of particular congregation members, when they learned the music, and the chain of associations awakened by it. Sometimes, unfortunately, text and music are in opposite modes and the conflicting messages cancel the potential strength of either element.

It is important for worship leaders, especially the pastor and musician, to know about these responses. One way to find out would be to take this map and apply it to an analysis of several services using past worship bulletins. You will need to be attentive not only to what is on the paper, but also to the way things were actually done and presented.

For example, those who are leading worship will often use words in ways that intrude upon the liturgy by giving instructions that are not necessary or by filling in the silences with chatter. Such behavior usually breaks the sense of prayer in the congregation. Worship leaders often act this way because they are anxious about their role and want to make sure the service "keeps rolling along smoothly." They want to keep in control of things, and often the congregation wants that too.

- What will happen if we call for silent prayer, and the silence lasts for more than a few seconds?
- What will happen if we simply allow the music to begin after we finish reading from the Bible, trusting that the Spirit will use the music to draw out the sense of the word without our intervening comments?
- What will happen if we use a simple gesture to invite people to stand rather than speaking it aloud like a stage director?

Generally speaking, this is what will happen: there will be a greater sense of anti-structure because the worship leaders will be exercising less direct personal control over the service. The structure will still be present in the order of the liturgy and in the established customs of the congregation, but we will not focus our attention on the ordering elements of worship. They will now serve to lead us to the boundary of mystery and wonder.

Part of the reason the leaders intrude themselves upon the spirit of prayer is their personal uneasiness about being up in front of the congregation. That is a phenomenon common to the leadership of any human group. But in the case of worship there is a deeper anxiety: the fear of encountering the holy, of being drawn toward the anti-structure where we are no longer in command as we surrender ourselves to God.

## Map Two: Oscillation Between Extra-dependence and Intra-dependence

The fear of the holy is present not only in the leaders, but also in the congregation. It is a fear well attested in the Bible, where to see the face of God is to die, where people meet angels in fear and trembling, where Moses takes off his shoes because he stands on holy ground. American culture, with the high value it places on being "self-made" and in control of one's destiny, amplifies the ancient fear we find in Scripture. Many congregations favor the worship leader who is chatty and intrusive on the spirit of prayer, and who will customarily begin a service with a cheery "Good morning, how are you?" instead of a call to worship or a remembrance of our sins or a hymn of adoration.

We may think that this is a small matter, that to disparage the use of "Good morning" is picky and ungracious. But, in fact, major issues are at stake here, not only for the vitality of worship, but also for the health of the world. There is a hunger for mystery that will not go away. If the church fails to satisfy this hunger by treating worship as nothing all that special—all we need to begin worshiping the Creator of the universe is a cheerful "Good morning"—then people will seek mystery in other practices.

The Grubb Institute in Great Britain has provided a theory of ritual that helps us to understand this phenomenon. It illumines in more detail what it means to be a liminal community that weaves back and forth between structure and anti-structure.

The Grubb theory describes two different modes of being. The first is intra-dependence, the state of depending upon ourselves. Most adults have to be intra-dependent most of their lives: the alarm clock goes off, we get up, get breakfast, and get going. We pour out energy to take care of ourselves and others.

Intra-dependence is demanding. We periodically need to change out of that role; we need to receive instead of give, to surrender control instead of take control, to become, in a word, "extra-dependent," to depend upon another. The church at worship invites people to become dependent upon the only One who is ultimately dependable: God. When worship "works," people find themselves renewed by the experience of extra-dependence so that they can return to their daily lives and take responsibility for using the gifts that God has given them. Even though people are not familiar with this theory, they frequently give witness to its validity by saying things like:

"I come to church to be inspired."

"I was fed by this service."

"That was a great service because we felt lifted up and renewed."

"Church is like a filling station: it gives me the fuel to get through another week."

Before we criticize the limitations of such statements, we need to recognize the profound yearning and practical pastoral truth that is in them: the cyclical need that God has planted in us to move back and forth between intra-dependence and extra-dependence. The Grubb Institute calls this "oscillation." Intrusive instructions from the leaders interrupt this process by keeping everything tightly controlled so that the service never leads us into a state of extra-dependence upon God. The result is eventually a feeling of boredom because worship becomes just one more intra-dependent activity in which we cease to expect an encounter with God. We go through the motions but our heart is not in it.

Thus an acquaintance of mine used to talk about how dull his church services were. I attended a few times and recall the incessant interruptions of the pastor, who kept announcing hymns and telling us what to do, when the bulletin and the actions of the people made it perfectly clear to me as a visitor what to do. That same acquaintance, however, would speak with religious enthusiasm about attending football games and the chill it gave him when, without announcement, the fans would send a wave around the stadium, as successive rows of them would stand and sit and a great roar would go up. He liked attending events as much for the ritual of cheering as for the sport itself. Attending the games provided a feeling of intense oneness with other fans that he never experienced in church.

There are dangers in the process of oscillation, of moving from intra-dependence to extra-dependence. The most obvious one is that we would cease to take responsibility for our lives and give ourselves to destructive ends. The films we have seen of the Hitler rallies in the 1930s come to mind immediately. Perhaps it is in part some dim awareness of this fear that makes us wary of extra-dependence.

There is also the danger that the theory of oscillation will lead people to consider worship as nothing more than an escape valve from their overburdened lives. They will come seeking the experience of extra-dependence as a way of tolerating situations that they need to be changing. They will not want to hear about the cries of the oppressed or of God's prophetic demand to do justice. They have come to give themselves into God's hands, not to take in hand the troubles of the world.

We have learned that it is the fear of this second danger that has often deterred worship leaders from allowing the service to lead the congregation toward extra-dependence. These leaders tell us that they want the service to be "relevant," and they often design the prayers, preaching, and musical selections all toward teaching the people about a particular social problem and challenging them to meet it. Although the intention is good, the result is often disappointing: the service neither empowers people for social witness nor gives them a sense of the holiness and wonder of God.

We compare these efforts with services we have attended in which people moved through the process of oscillation and left church filled with power to carry on the corporate and personal witness of the church. We think, for example, of an African American inner-city church, which is known for its fervent congregational song and prayer. The opening is never a cheery, "Good morning," but always a reading from the Psalms or other Scripture that immediately focuses our attention on God, not on ourselves. The dignity of the leaders and the choir suggests to any visitor that something momentous and sacred is about to happen. The service moves inexorably toward extra-dependence, often captured in the slow and extended singing of a hymn, frequently repeating the refrain again and again such as "I surrender all to Jesus" or "Melt me, mold me, fill me, use me." There is no rush to bring it to an end prematurely.

Observing this period of extra-dependence in the service, a stranger unfamiliar with the church's mission might conclude that the congregation was indulging in irrelevance and passivity, confirming our worst fears about the process of oscillation. But, in fact, the church is one of the most dynamic forces in the neighborhood and city addressing the social problems of food, housing, medical care, racism, and drugs. Their worship feeds their life as a community and their mission to the world. They attain these goals, not by making their services chatty and relevant, but by entrusting themselves to God who gives them strength to do the work of love and justice.

This church's witness, and the witness of many others like it, demonstrates the power of moving between intra- and extra-dependence. David Newman has provided us with a phrase that sums up the character of healthy oscillation in the title of his book, *Worship as Praise and Empowerment*. Newman observes that

> Worship as *praise only* can exalt God at the expense of human beings, thereby diminishing their responsibility for their own lives. It seeks a sphere of human existence that is untouched by, and thereby acquiescing in, the dominant forces at work in human society. The voices that are crying out for justice not only in society at large, but in the church itself, are left unheard. Worship ought also to empower. But worship as *empowerment only*, without praise, is put at the service of individual need as a private indulgence, something to get by on but only useful while the need remains. Or it loses itself in the cause of particular conflicting movements in society, pursuing this end and that, but always fashioning a god only to serve whatever ends are in view. A god that is put at our human disposal is always an idol. Worship, therefore, must include both praise and empowerment.[3]

The need to interweave praise and empowerment in our worship reminds us of a pastor who decided that after the reading from the Hebrew Scriptures, the congregation should no longer sing "Glory be to the Father and to the Son and to the Holy Ghost." The pastor explained that the words unfairly Christianized those ancient passages. And in light of the church's history of anti-Semitism, it has an obligation to allow those Scriptures to speak without having a much later trinitarian formula imposed upon them. Although his theological argument made sense, the pastor never found another placement for the "Gloria," but simply dropped it altogether. The people were outraged because as they said, "We sing it so well. We don't need our books. We love the way we know it by heart and the way the organ supports us on it."

Not until the pastor learned about anti-structure and extra-dependence did it become clear why the people were so adamant about not giving up their "Gloria." What they were saying in effect was: "You are taking away one of the few times in the service when we can give ourselves completely to God's praise, when we move beyond structure, when we become extra-dependent." Once the pastor realized this, it was possible to find a more appropriate placement for the "Gloria," one that honored the pastor's principle of treating the Hebrew Scriptures with integrity and the people's need to sing the "Gloria."

Once they realized together what the congregation's deeper need was, they decided to begin to learn other musical responses that would allow them to join in singing to God without the encumbrance of books. As the congregation's repertoire of beloved memorized responses increased, they became less rigid about the one they originally fought to keep because they now had a number of ways to express their extra-dependence.

What about your congregation?

- How well do you balance extra-dependence and intra-dependence?
- Which elements provide one or the other?
- What current practices of worship leadership encourage or disrupt the process of oscillation?

105

• Does your worship provide both praise and empowerment? Why or why not?

This is the point of using these maps: not to blame one another for what is wrong in our worship, but to identify the root cause of our difficulty, and to consider how it can be addressed.

## Map Three: Different Personality Types

I (Tom) remember the first time my wife and I went to a wallpaper store. After looking through four or five books of patterns my head was swimming and I could not remember in which book any pattern I liked was to be found. Yet I can usually go to the stacks in the library and pull down a book I have not read for years, and find the passage I want. I am a word person, and words stay with me.

My wife, who is an attorney and also adept with words, has the additional gift of a keen eye for color and pattern. While I was ready to leave the store, she was having a wonderful time plowing on through more books, remembering a print she had seen twenty minutes earlier that was similar, though the greens were a little brighter. Her memory for color and shape and her energy to keep looking at a wealth of patterns amazed me.

The contrast between my wife and me is typical of the enormous variations in perceiving and responding to the world that are present in a congregation. People bring these differences to worship. Some will be very upset if words are changed because their primary way of dealing with the world is through words. But others will not care. They are primarily engaged through what they see or the way they and others move their bodies, and words will be less important.

Attempts to determine which senses and faculties are appropriate for the expressive actions of worship is a dilemma that haunts the history of Christian worship. Without recounting the entire story of the struggle here,[4] it strikes us from the way the problem periodically re-emerges that there is some force—we believe it is the Spirit of God—that keeps seeking to bring the whole human person into the act of worship.

There have been periods in the church's history when certain senses and faculties were favored over others and were lifted up as the superior or only way to approach God in worship. We think especially of the reformers of the sixteenth century, who stressed the use of the ear as the "gate to heaven." If we have been raised in such a tradition and its history is precious to us, we may consider those reformers' statements to be the last and authoritative word on the subject. However, recent scholarship has helped us realize that the nearly exclusive emphasis upon "hearing God's word" needs to be examined in the light of the historical conditions that gave rise to such a view, especially the liturgical practices and the decoration of the interior space of the churches in that period:

> A balanced equilibrium between language for instruction and clarification and visual images to direct and increase devotional piety had eluded the late-medieval Roman church.
>
> In dramatic contrast to the verbal impoverishment of worship, the engagement of vision had never been stronger.[5]

In other words, the Reformers' extreme emphasis on hearing was a response to the church's extreme emphasis on seeing. This violent shift in approaches met with the same mixed reception that is familiar to anyone who has tried to reform worship. One person said of a church that had been stripped of its overcluttered and extravagantly decorated interior, "There was nothing at all inside, and it was hideous"; while another wrote of such changes, "We have churches which are positively luminous; the walls are beautifully white."[6]

The intensity of the conflict that sounds in these words from the sixteenth century continues to sound in many of our churches today. What resources do we have to help us approach these differences in ways that can vitalize the church's worship so that it engages "all of us for all of God"?[7]

One resource is the first and greatest commandment, that we are to love God with all our heart, mind, soul, and strength—a phrase indicating the entirety of who we are. We often spiritualize our understanding of some of these terms and lose the material force of these words, forgetting that

> the ancient Hebrews did not make a sharp distinction between physical and psychic powers and tended to attribute psychological functions to certain organs of the body. Of all such organs the heart was the chief; it was the innermost spring of individual life, the ultimate source of all its physical, intellectual, emotional, and volitional energies, and consequently the part of man [and woman] through which [they] normally achieved contact with the divine.[8]

There is a holistic character to this first command that we have lost, but which suggests the importance of bringing our entire selves to worship. Our efforts to achieve a balanced engagement of the senses in worship represents our desire to keep the first and greatest commandment.

This theological perspective is reinforced by our increased understanding of the way different people perceive and respond to the world. In recent years a number of writers have used the Myers-Briggs personality types to analyze why different people find themselves drawn to different styles of prayer.

One of the basic polarities in the Myers-Briggs test is between sensing and intuitive persons. "Sensing personalities have an immediate recognition of their surroundings equaled by no other personality. They quickly become aware of the color of the walls, the texture of the floor, the lighting, etc. . . . Intuitive personalities are concerned more with the future than with the present. They are never quite present in the present."[9]

It sounds like the difference between my wife and me in the wallpaper store! Or like the differences we experienced at a hymn festival in a large church with people from many other regions. Afterward, someone remarked about the messy look of the chancel, particularly all the chairs that were being stored on each side of the altar steps. Another person responded, "What chairs? I did not see any chairs. I just noticed that there is not much reverberation in the room. The organ sounded muffled."

Simply knowing that people have different ways of perceiving the world and that they bring these to their experience of worship can free us from making absolute statements about the rightness of one over the other. If our role is to provide leadership for our church's worship, then it is necessary that we consider those who process and respond in ways different from our own:

> All indicators point to a close relationship between our innate temperament and the type of prayer best suited to our needs. Introverts will prefer a form of prayer different from Extroverts. Intuitives approach God from a point of view different from Sensers. Feelers pray in a different way from Thinkers. Judging persons want structure in their prayer life, while Perceiving persons want flexibility. As we grow in maturity and learn to make good use of all

our abilities in functioning and relating, our prayer life should become richer. While we may still prefer the type of prayer that matches our natural temperament, we should familiarize ourselves with the other forms of prayer that have been developed over the centuries.[10]

We have often witnessed the dramatic difference between people's reactions to various forms of corporate prayer depending upon their natural temperament. We recall, for example, two men sitting next to each other at a conference. Earlier in the day we had learned to pray the Lord's Prayer to some new music that was accompanied by simple physical gestures interpreting the words—raising arms upward on the word "heaven," cupping one's hands together and holding them out on "daily bread," and so forth. Both men were in their fifties and longtime members of the same church. One of them was moved by the gestures because they had opened him to the meaning of the prayer. The other found the gestures intrusive, obscuring the "thought of the prayer." However, this second man had the grace to be glad that the gestures had been helpful to his friend. Without such grace our personality types can become excuses for not recognizing that

we need to develop some of our less favored characteristics if we want to grow more aware and to appreciate the value of others whose personality types are different from our own. Such development may even facilitate spiritual growth, encouraging us to pursue some spiritual approaches we would normally find ineffective.[11]

If we avoid such development it is not only our personal spiritual growth that may suffer, but the church's as well, especially if we remain closed and judgmental toward those who display a completely different way of perceiving and being. We think here of people who have posted their Myers-Briggs personality type on bulletin boards or desks and then excused themselves from larger community obligations on the basis of their natural temperament. If we all followed this practice, the church would swiftly devolve into a new series of tribes: the intuitives versus the feelers, the feelers versus the thinkers. In fact, this often happens as people disparage the desires of personality types that are different from their own with pejorative titles: "touchy feely types," "head trippers," "aesthetes," and so on.

Such labeling nurtures and reinforces the fragmentation of the community. It becomes a way of conveniently forgetting that the gospel presents us with obligations that are greater than our natural affinities, and one of them is to maintain the church as the body of Christ, with all its conflicted variations in personality types. Although we will never know for certain, it is not irresponsible to speculate that such conflicts fed the apostle Paul's detailed metaphor of the body and its various senses:

> If the foot would say, "Because I am not a hand, I do not belong to the body," that would not make it any less a part of the body. And if the ear would say, "Because I am not an eye, I do not belong to the body," that would not make it any less a part of the body. If the whole body were an eye, where would the hearing be? If the whole body were hearing, where would the sense of smell be? But as it is, God arranged the members in the body, each one of them, as he chose. If all were a single member, where would the body be? As it is, there are many members, yet one body. (1 Corinthians 12:15-20)

Walk into your worship area as a worship committee and review what happens on a Sunday morning.
- What ways of perceiving and responding does your service favor?
- Which does it neglect or ignore altogether?
- What kind of personality type will be most at home?
- Which will be most left out?

If it turns out that your church needs to give more attention to the "eye" of the body of Christ—and this is the case in the majority of churches with which we have worked—do not rush prematurely to a solution. If we have never developed the art of attentive looking and visualizing, then we should not assume that just because our eyes work we can "see." We may first need the assistance of a visual artist or designer, someone who has professionally honed skills of judging proportion, depth, texture, color, and shape. We are not necessarily talking about rebuilding the church or radically altering its interior. There may be simple changes that would enrich our services.

Gregor T. Goethals describes the potential for artists and local congregations entering into "a collaborative, searching process" that is based upon the realization that "Before images and objects were 'Art,' they were essentially the human quest for metaphors to understand life processes."[12]

We have experienced that "collaborative, searching process" in the life of our own community, which resulted in an inexpensive but effective new use of an old space. Prior to hiring the artist, we had nearly despaired of using our school auditorium for worship because the stage dominated one end of the room and seemed to keep drawing our eyes there even when we placed the chairs in a circle. Yet we were eager to be able to use the auditorium since the fixed pews of our chapel precluded doing more flexible kinds of services. Our situation was similar to many churches that need to move their services into parlors and fellowship halls to save on heating expenses during the winter. They find themselves frustrated by an environment that is not conducive to prayer and wonder how to change it.

The artist we hired did several things with us before he made any proposals. First he attended many of our services, both those in our neo-Gothic chapel and those in the auditorium. He talked with us about what it was like for him as a stranger in our worship, asking questions, pointing out things we had never noticed. He presented a slide show of different ancient, medieval, and post-Reformation worship churches, and then pictures of contemporary public spaces, sacred and secular. The response to the pictures was overwhelming. People who had spent nearly their entire educational and religious life enmeshed in words were astonished that their eyes could tell them things they never knew.

As the artist approached the end of the process he invited a cross-section of the community to draw pictures symbolizing their highest hopes for our worship and then gave them an opportunity to present and interpret their drawings. On the basis of all of this interaction and instruction, he drew up what seemed so simple we could hardly believe we had not thought of it ourselves.

He placed a dramatically large hanging on the inside wall of the auditorium, which is at right angles to the stage. The hanging took the themes from our drawings and reduced them to a few striking lines and colors. A member of the congregation sewed it together following the design of the artist. The hanging, rather than the stage, now became the focal point of the room. Chairs were placed "three-quarters in the round," some facing the hanging directly and others at right angles to the wall. In the middle of the space the artist positioned a large table and two candles.

The first time people walked into the auditorium for worship there were audible cries of "how beautiful." The artist had listened to us carefully and had then drawn on his special gifts to come up with a design and arrangement that expressed who we were as a community.

Although we continued to enjoy the arrangement of the room, the hanging fell into disfavor when a new generation of students arrived, and it is now seldom used. This would probably not bother the artist since one of the things he taught us is that churches need to have a room set aside as a museum. They can use it to retire hangings and other objects when they are no longer the expression of the community's faith. This provides a way to avoid the clutter that often accumulates in our worship spaces when we are reluctant to remove something because simple disposal would strike us as irreverent.

This attention to the visual aspects of our worship is far more than a luxury. Gregor T. Goethals sets her discussion of religion and art in the context of how the mass media make meaning through images that function as symbols,[13] often representing values that are at odds with the gospel. Part of the witness of worship is to provide an alternative symbolic world, one which calls into question the assumptions of the media world. As important as words are, they alone cannot fill this purpose, especially in a culture where images are such a significant part of the communication of our world view. Worship that is exclusively or overwhelmingly verbal cannot hope to engage a visual world. As our experience with the artist demonstrates, this does not necessarily mean making changes that are beyond your church's budget or the reach of your people's imaginations. But it does imply that each of us will stretch beyond our personality type in order to fulfill the first commandment and to encompass more completely the apostle Paul's vision of the whole body of Christ.

## Map Four: Different Levels of History

Most families have photograph albums or slides or nowadays videotape collections of their important celebrations. The ever-popular theme in these collections is recording the big events of childhood. Once we are grown up it is fascinating—and yes, sometimes embarrassing—to look back at these pictures and to think that the small child with chocolate all over the face and looking out of the picture with delighted eyes is you, now a respected adult. We treasure these pictures because they give us a sense of who we are, where we have come from, and what has helped to shape our present lives and character.

I recall a heartbreaking letter in the newspaper from a woman whose house had been robbed. She told the thieves to keep everything except one small ring that was worth nothing on the market, but that was priceless to her because her father had bought it for her as a novelty at the state fair when she was a little girl. She did not want to lose the symbol that gave her a tangible sense of the past.

What is true of individuals is also true of communities. They need to hold on to the memories of the past in order to understand who they are. If they forget, then they will lose their identity and sense of purpose. The Hebrew poet who was exiled to Babylon gives poignant expression to this insight: "If I forget you, O Jerusalem, let my right hand wither!" (Psalm 137:5). The right hand was the symbol for strength in ancient belief, and Jerusalem represented a complex web of associations, including the memory of worship in the temple. To forget that past would be to lose the essential vitality of what it meant to be a believer in the Lord.

Most of us have probably been involved with an organization that at some time or another began to lose sight of its goals. When this happens, the membership grows restless. Many of them drop out or resist the work that they once did gladly. But sometimes the leaders and the members will call themselves to account and say: "Now when this organization was founded. . . ." Then there may follow stories of the beginning of things and of the outstanding members and leaders of the past, and a restatement of purpose and philosophy. This recounting of history can provide an infusion of energy to help the organization find its way again.

Yet built into any act of memory is the danger that we will idealize the past and only consider as authentic that which is historical. Most of us have also been involved in organizations like this. We say of such a group, "They are living in the past. They have lost contact with the way things really are. They have no vision for the future."

The observation of human organizations reveals that groups need to maintain both their memories of the past and their visionary capacities for the present and the future. This is as true for the church as it is for any other group.

A significant part of Christian worship is the continual renewal of the community's primary memories: what God has done for us through creation, the Exodus, the prophets, Christ, and the ongoing work of the Spirit. If this memory is allowed to fade or its retelling becomes merely rote, then the worship of the church will flounder. It will be like any other organization that forgets its past and begins to wander aimlessly.

But at the same time the church can never afford to limit itself to expressions of faith from the past. As Christ tells us in the Gospel of John, the Spirit blows as free as the wind. To shut ourselves off to new motions of the Spirit is as great a sin as neglecting the past.

How to hold together memory and vision, past and present, tradition and innovation is a struggle that often comes to a crisis when we gather the tribes for Sunday morning worship. The sharpest tribal conflict in many churches is the division between those who would be glad to stay with things as they have "always been" and those who would be pleased to dispense with tradition in order to be relevant now.

The problem with both of these positions is that neither one accurately reflects reality. The only way the church has "always been" is always changing so that to hold on to one way of prayer and song is in fact to dishonor the past and tradition by ignoring its dynamic character. This mistreatment of the past results in making it seem stale and dull, incapable of conveying any redeeming power to people in the present.

On the other hand, we have observed the disillusionment of people who were originally attracted by the idea of completely innovative worship. What starts with a burst of enthusiasm begins to wear thin because people cannot come up with an endless supply of new ideas and because ritual by nature is repetitive. Innovators who get rid of one tradition usually settle into their own, which often fails to stand the test of time. The new songs that were so appealing upon their introduction grow tiresome for lack of musical substance. They may not hold the same meaning for the new members as they did for the founders. The absence of prayers, words, and music inherited from ancient tradition gives the service a flimsy feeling, as if faith and worship were simply one more passing fashion among the myriad fads that come and go.

There are resources for thinking about the relationship of tradition and innovation that can rescue us from the distortions of antiquarianism and faddishness. One major resource is the dynamic understanding of memory that prevails in the Bible. Memory is not presented as the simple recall of events that happened once upon a time long ago. Instead, history is understood as an urgent word for the present. We can see this clearly in the way the psalmist describes the stories of the past and his reason for recounting them:

> Give ear, O my people, to my teaching;
>> incline your ears to the words of my mouth.
> I will open my mouth in a parable;
>> I will utter dark sayings from of old,

things that we have heard and known,
　　that our ancestors have told us.
We will not hide them from their children;
　　we will tell to the coming generation
the glorious deeds of the LORD, and his might,
　　and the wonders that he has done.

He established a decree in Jacob,
　　and appointed a law in Israel,
which he commanded our ancestors
　　to teach to their children;
that the next generation might know them,
　　the children yet unborn,
and rise up and tell them to their children,
　　so that they should set their hope in God,
and not forget the works of God,
　　but keep his commandments;
and that they should not be like their ancestors,
　　a stubborn and rebellious generation,
a generation whose heart was not steadfast,
　　whose spirit was not faithful to God.
　　　　　　　　　　　　　　　　(Psalm 78:1-8)

The psalmist does not romanticize the past. Instead, the psalmist is forthright about the failings of the ancestors, "whose heart was not steadfast,/whose spirit was not faithful to God." But at the same time the psalmist realizes the importance of that past to the present and future in order that subsequent generations "should set their hope in God,/and not forget the works of God,/but keep his commandments." The psalm is just one illustration of the general principle

that for the Hebrew the recollection of the past means that what is recalled becomes a present reality, which in turn controls the will. . . .
Memory revives faith. In turn, in the cultic ceremonies themselves Israel remembers her ancient story, the works

of God, his marvelous deeds in times past. Thus cult is sacred memory becoming sacred reality and life for the participants. The bearing of all this on the role of remembrance in the words for the institution of the Lord's Supper (Luke 22:19; 1 Corinthians 11:24-25) is clear. Through the elements Christians are to remember Jesus Christ, but it follows from this meal that Christ is not merely remembered, but becomes a real presence through the remembrance. Their remembrances are thus the medium for the holy reality of Jesus Christ, and in this holy reality the life of the spirit is quickened and revived.[14]

Edward Schillebeeckx has devised a model for the interpretation of history that can help us maintain in our worship the dynamic function of memory that we find in the Bible. In his book, *Jesus, An Experiment in Christology,* Schillebeeckx describes a process of cultural change in which at least three planes are discernible. These are explained as three concentric circles rotating on a single axis.

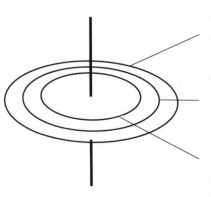

*Ephemeral history:*
brief and rapidly
expiring

*Conjunctural history:*
more comprehensive;
slower tempo of change

*Structural history:*
time span of centuries;
almost bordering on
nonmovement

Structural history (the innermost circle) includes the "classic," widely accepted ideas. This would embrace set prayers and deeply established congregational hymns and music, what people often call the "golden oldies" in the ecumenical literature of Christian song. It would be difficult to imagine their ever disappearing from common use.

Conjunctural history is understood to move somewhat faster around the slower moving structural history. Contained in it are those elements which are either in the process of becoming structural history or are at least enjoying temporary acceptability. Examples would include the recovery by many Protestant denominations of the service of remembering our baptismal vows. This ancient service had fallen into disuse because of theological debates in earlier centuries. But now a renewed appreciation for the sacrament of baptism and its implications for the ministry of the whole church has led to its reinstitution. We cannot call the service "ephemeral" because it bears an ancient heritage, but it has not yet become "structural" in the churches where it is being introduced. So it falls in the category of "conjunctural."

Recent hymnals provide another example. Many of them include musical settings that once were standard and well known, then fell out of favor, but now are being revived as a way of giving new life to beloved texts. They are not yet in the congregation's standard repertoire, but they represent more than a passing fad or they would have been lost completely.

The outer circle, which is moving and changing most rapidly, is described as ephemeral history. New elements of worship enter the process through this orbit and may pass into the conjunctural area or may be spun away never to be seen or heard again. Examples would include: a youth group that goes to a church camp and brings back a ritual using balloons, which delights everyone as a special celebration, but which never becomes a regular part of worship; a series of banners made by the Sunday school, which are bright and festive when they are first brought in, but a few weeks later have lost their communicative power; a song that people bring back from a religious retreat, which lifts everyone's heart with its joy, but which is too simple to hold people's interest with repeated singing.

In Schillebeeckx's model, ephemeral history is an *essential* part of the historical process. It serves the whole by functioning as a point of entry for elements that aspire to influence history. Every age produces an enormous surfeit of hymnody, religious song, prayer, and ritual innovations. There is no way all of it will stand the test of time But without it nothing new would ever come into the church.

It is also important to stress that simply because something is structural history does not mean that it cannot be critically reviewed. When we look at the church's past with the same unblinking gaze that the psalmist fixed on Israel, we see that the structural history of the church is often entangled with sexism, racism, anti-Semitism, and the mistreatment of those with disabling conditions. For us who love the church, this is often a source of great pain, and there is the temptation to hide from the ugly truth. But we believe in God who calls us to justice, and therefore we will work to free our worship from patterns that are destructive to any group of human beings. Some of the things that may initially seem like nothing more than "ephemeral history" because they challenge "structural history" will turn out in the long run to be a manifestation of the Spirit working to purify and revitalize the church.

A large part of the conflict in the revitalization of the church is therefore a theological debate about what is central to its identity and what is not. There is no map or chart that can effortlessly solve these great debates. They are a necessary part of the church's life. There has never been a period of history when they have not been going on, and there is no reason to believe that our age and the ages to come will be any different.

What the three-tiered model of history provides is a way of assessing how well our church is maintaining the dynamic function of memory in the worship of our local church. It helps us to visualize the fact that being traditional or being innovative are not polar opposites, that they are aspects of a simultaneous and continuous process. Once we understand this, then we are no longer reduced to either/or arguments. Will our services be traditional or will they be innovative?

Instead, we are led to a much more productive line of liturgical planning. We begin to consider how the balloons or the banners or the song of the moment can be a powerful complement to the structural and conjunctural elements of our worship. We do not assume that every such innovation will become structural and take over all our services.

However, if something appears to have potentially lasting value, we may keep it long enough to become part of our conjunctural history. For example, many of the ancient rituals that our denominations have now revived as "new" liturgical resources will require repeated use to make a sound judgment of their place in our congregation's life. Likewise, the variety of ways we now have for singing the psalms cannot be dismissed after a single effort. Congregations that try such things over an extended period of time often discover that their resistance turns to acceptance. What seemed like "just some new thing to learn" moves from ephemeral to conjunctural and finally structural history.

We will not see these shifts happen instantly. They become apparent as we evaluate the overall practice of our liturgical life and ask ourselves these critical questions:

• Are we providing enough structural history to maintain the identity of our church?

- Are we being open enough to ephemeral history so that we can receive its refreshment and the new leading of the Spirit?
- Do we give adequate time for some of our innovations to become part of conjunctural history where we can see if they bear the test of repeated use?

## Map Five: Developing a Common Language

Any group that is involved in a common task develops its own vocabulary. Sometimes this is frustrating to outsiders because they cannot understand what is being said. Everything seems in code. Yet to the members of the group it is helpful. It facilitates clear and precise communication.

Often it is the lack of such clear terms that frustrates our discussions about worship. When something goes right or something goes wrong, we are often reduced to exasperation because we do not know how to name the source of our response. Having available basic concepts and terms that we share with each other can help us to locate and articulate the cause of our reaction more precisely.

We have already begun developing such a vocabulary through the study of our first four maps. You now have the following terms to draw upon in analyzing the worship life of your church:

- structure
- anti-structure
- intra-dependence
- extra-dependence
- personality types and their relationship to worship
- structural history
- conjunctural history
- ephemeral history.

Having a list of concepts like this helps us to see that what we experience in worship, both its joys and frustrations, is not merely random and chaotic. There are patterns that we can identify; principles that we can name.

But since everyone will not learn or remember terms as technical as these, we now present another list of words taken from common speech that provide a useful vocabulary for talking about liturgical matters. These are words that will be helpful to pastors, musicians, and worship committees when they are trying to evaluate a particular service or to aid other members of the congregation in expressing their delight or displeasure about something:

- proportion
- appropriateness
- flow
- congruence
- shape or direction
- inclusivity.

We introduce each word with a story to make clear how it functions as a term of liturgical description. As you read these stories take time to remember your own experiences as a worshiper, which are clarified by the use of the term.

### Proportion

The service was featuring a new hymn text played to a favorite tune of the congregation's. It was a special celebration, and the church was packed. People were singing their hearts out. Before the last stanza the organ began to play an interlude that would let the organist pull out all the stops for a grand finale. The congregation was used to this practice, and they waited for the cadence that would indicate that they should join in the last verse. But soon the hymn tune had given way to complex fugal material, which in turn led to an extensive exercise in modulation. The interlude went on and on, taking several minutes for the hymn tune to return. When the congregation was eventually permitted to begin the last stanza, the spirit was gone from their singing, and afterward people grumbled coming out of church.

The interlude was not the right "proportion" to the hymn. It overwhelmed the congregation's song by being too grand, too long. It might have been stunning in an organ recital, but it failed as an act of prayer.

We can tell the same story about sermons that have gone on long after they have made their point or an announcement that became a second homily or any other liturgical action that did not fit the service because it was too long or too short, because it was the wrong proportion for what it was supposed to do and be in the service.

Proportion extends not only to the words and actions of liturgy, but also to the symbols and objects of worship. For example, when we were working with the artist who showed us how to use our auditorium as an effective worship space, he brought in two sets of slides: one was of fountains in airports and shopping malls, the other was of church baptismal furnishings and pools. In the secular public spaces water flowed in abundance; in the churches there were often a few drops or a tiny bowl. The proportion of the water in the churches communicated a stinginess that was the exact opposite of the extravagant grace that God is showing us in baptism.

## Appropriateness

A minister who was eager to meet a congregation's expressed desire for a greater sense of closeness opened a service with the words, "I love you, and so does God. Now turn and tell that to someone next to you." There was a long, awkward pause among the people, and then most of them dutifully turned to one another and mumbled the words, many of them with their eyes cast down and obviously embarrassed.

The minister's intention was understandable, but the means of achieving it was inappropriate for many reasons. First of all, the statement makes the leader's love, rather than God's love, primary. Knowing how human love comes and goes, it will never be an adequately reassuring reason for gathering us to worship.

Furthermore, the sentence confuses different levels of language. "I love you" spoken to another human being is a statement of intimate feeling. It is not something most people speak aloud in public, but something reserved for more private occasions. The minister put his people in an awkward position by asking them to say what they felt was inappropriate. They did it mechanically because they did not want to appear ungracious, but they resented how they felt compelled to speak words that were not appropriate to the setting. Thus the well-intentioned effort to build community had the opposite effect: creating an even greater sense of distance and awkwardness between people.

Appropriateness is something that varies from local church to local church and even among groups within the same congregation. We can never assume that what was appropriate in one setting is appropriate in the next. For example, I recently talked to an elderly woman from a congregation with a large number of widows her age or older. A new pastor had come and introduced the custom of having each congregation member tear a piece of bread from the communion loaf to feed one another. He recalled how this had increased the sense of oneness in Christ in the last congregation he served. However, in this case many of the elderly had arthritis or weakness in their hands that made it painful and in some cases nearly impossible to break the bread. Instead of increasing closeness, the new practice amplified people's anxiety that they would drop the bread and desecrate a sacred moment.

Sometimes the sense of what is appropriate can stifle legitimate reform. One way to handle this is to introduce new music and liturgical practices on less formal occasions of worship, for example, at church suppers or on retreats. The fact that you are not in the church itself will often allow you greater flexibility. It feels appropriate to experiment outside of the usual place of worship. If what you introduce takes hold in the hearts of people, they may then come to see it as appropriate to their regular liturgy.

## Flow

My wife and I were visiting a church as strangers one Easter Sunday. The pastor had obviously not thought out the beginning of the service. He started by speaking as a teacher to school children: "It is traditional for Christians on Easter to greet each other in the following way:

'Alleluia. Christ is risen.'

'The Lord is risen indeed. Alleluia.'"

He then had the congregation repeat the greeting and followed it with these words: "And so you do that. Now let's see. Yes, the hymn is, 'Jesus Christ Is Risen Today.'" The entire impression was of someone slowly reciting a recipe comprised of slightly questionable ingredients. There was no sense at all of how the announcement of Christ's resurrection would flow into glad and heartfelt song.

How to design and lead a service so that it flows becomes particularly crucial when there are special rites that are not a part of our usual liturgy or when there is a need to have people move about without the intrusion of spoken directions.

We were recently impressed by a visit to a university chapel where there was an ecumenical congregation with many visitors because summer school was in session. The ushers had been taught clear, simple gestures to direct congregation members when and where to come forward during the Lord's Supper. Even though we were strangers, we were able to participate without any hesitation or uneasiness because of the careful thought the leaders had given to keeping the liturgical action flowing.

### Congruence

Congruence is related to flow and is often a function of how well the music fits with the other elements of the service. We recall a pastor who told us a story of perfect *in*congruence. Although he and his musician usually consulted carefully, they had not been able to get together for several weeks. In response to requests from the congregation, the pastor was preaching about personal prayer on this particular Sunday. His sermon included material on the spiritual discipline of waiting upon God in silence, and the sermon had concluded on a subdued note. The anthem that followed, however, included a special accompaniment of trumpet and timpani! It was not a deliberate refutation of the sermon, but a mixup based on a simple lack of communication between musician and pastor. This does not mean that there should never be striking contrasts in a service, but when they occur they should be congruent with the development of the service.

Congruence also is a way of describing how well the musical setting of a hymn matches the meaning of the text or how successfully the words of a prayer fulfill its function in the service. Here, for example, is a prayer that was submitted to a committee that was revising its denomination's liturgical texts:

O God our Ultimate Concern, who is more likely down than out, and who reveals the void of his Being more clearly in our questions than in our answers; Teach us to communicate relevantly with each other across the sacred-secular dichotomy of our existential predicament. Establish authentic I-Thou relationships in the ambiguous context of our pluralistic society. Sensitize us to the hidden agenda of our peer groups in terms of meaningful ego-satisfactions. And help us to confront all disturbed and disadvantaged persons with underlying concern for the paradoxical reality of their interpersonal dynamics. In the Name of our mutual responsibility and interdependence in the Body of Christ. *Amen.*[15]

The prayer, rejected by the committee because of its tangled language, illustrates in a dramatic fashion one of the major incongruences of many prayers offered by leaders on behalf of the congregation: they are sermons or theological statements masked as prayers. It is not that sermons or theological statements are wrong, but that they are a different genre of religious speech. They are addressed by human beings to other human beings, while prayer is addressed to God.

Another form of incongruence is action that obscures rather than enhances the meaning of some element in the service. We think here of a service in which a congregation was asked to sing a new hymn and simultaneously provide gestures that interpreted the refrain. It was a congregation that welcomed the use of such gestures, and it was an occasion when the new hymn was perfectly appropriate. But putting the two together made both gesture and song impossible. People began to lift their hands only to draw them back midway through the gesture when they realized that they needed to hold the song sheet closer in order to see the new words and music. Then realizing that the gesture was still continuing, they jerked their hands back into motion to catch up with the leader. The hymn was about being one in Christ, but the mad waving of song sheets and the awkward vacillation between gesturing and singing made the experience incongruent with the intention.

To achieve congruence, then, we need to be attentive to two concerns: the relationship of each element in the service to what precedes and follows it, and to how well the language, musical idiom, or action of a particular rite fills its intended function.

### Shape or Direction

One of the most outstanding characteristics of a satisfying ritual is that it has a distinctive pattern. We do not experience it as simply a random stringing together of prayers, actions, songs, and words, but as a continuous action leading us in a particular direction. All traditions have some established underlying pattern to their worship. It may be recorded in a prayer book, printed in a bulletin, or held in the community's memory and passed on orally.

However, simply knowing the pattern and filling in the parts will not ensure a sense of shape to the service. For example, if every hymn is of exactly the same proportion—all of them strong hymns of praise or all of them hymns of personal devotion—the service will feel immobile; we are putting out energy singing but are covering the same ground again and again.

The way a service closes is crucial to our sense of liturgical direction. We recall a story of a pastor who wanted to encourage the entire congregation to attend the adult education program following worship. He decided that instead of giving a benediction at the end of the service, he would save the final blessing until after the education program. Even those congregation members who were already committed to attending the education program were furious. There was universal revolt because without the benediction, the people did not feel they could leave their pews. The entire service lacked that sense of completion and empowerment for ministry that is conveyed by a benediction. The pastor realized that he had misjudged the situation and restored the benediction to its rightful place.

We can understand the forces at work in this story even more completely if we combine the concept of liturgical shape or direction with our earlier discussion of the theory of oscillation between intra-dependence and extra-dependence. In the case of this church, the Eucharist was celebrated every Sunday with the people coming forward to receive the elements. Such an action involves extreme extra-dependence: we depend entirely upon Christ to feed us. But having been fed we must return to the world to take responsibility for the ministries entrusted to us. We need to go out in an intra-dependent state. If we are going to attend adult education we will need to be intra-dependent, because learning requires our taking responsibility for testing new ideas. Thus, the shape or direction of the liturgy is important not only to the act of worship itself, but also to the church's other ministries. A service marked by congruence and proportion and flowing clearly toward the final empowerment of the people is a service that feeds the church's whole ministry.

## Inclusivity

There is a story that we have now heard from so many pastors and laypeople in recent years that we no longer associate it with one particular congregation. The plot, with variations, is always the same. Someone or some group in the church suggests that the church needs to be made accessible to those who have difficulty coming because the church stairs are a barrier. There is resistance initially, but once the ramps or other helpful devices are put in place, the congregation is astounded at their effect.

People who use walkers or wheelchairs, people who have heart or asthmatic conditions begin to show up for service. And not only this, but also many others who had originally objected to the ramps are seen to use them!

We find in this common story a revelation about what happens when the church dares to become more inclusive: those who were left out come in and those who were already present acknowledge needs that before went unrecognized.

We extend this principle of inclusivity to every aspect of the church's worship:

- the adequate lighting that is required for people to see the words of hymns and prayers
- the maintenance of a quality acoustical instrument, which is necessary to supporting the song of the whole congregation
- the hospitality shown by ushers and other members of the congregation, which will enable strangers to join in the worship wholeheartedly
- a variety of musical idioms that not only touches the variety of tastes in the congregation, but that is also inclusive of the church's witness through the centuries
- language that makes it clear no one is excluded or judged less worthy of God's grace because of gender, race, or disabling condition.

We realize that some of these items will meet severe resistance in many congregations. But we are convinced from observing churches that have embodied these principles that the resultant sense of being the body of Christ is worth the struggle. Christianity is a religion that claims "the word has become flesh," not just kind thoughts or good intentions, but flesh. Therefore it is never adequate for the church simply to talk about grace, justice, compassion, and community. The church must live them, and if it does not live them when it gathers to praise God, then it will not live them in the world.

# Three Images of Renewing Worship

As you review our list of terms, you will discover that it is by no means exhaustive, and you may find yourself coming up with your own words. Write them down, talk about them in your worship committee. The goal is to develop a working vocabulary that can facilitate clear and constructive conversation, especially during those times when you are most frustrated and you need to be as accurate as possible.

But no list of terms is in itself adequate. Just as there is a need to balance various polarities in our services, so too our thinking and speaking about worship need to balance analytical thought with imagining and dreaming. As Amos N. Wilder has observed:

> It is at the level of the imagination that the fateful issues of our new world-experience must first be mastered. It is here that culture and history are broken, and here that the church is polarized. Old words do not reach across the new gulfs, and it is only in vision and oracle that we can chart the unknown and new-name the creatures.[16]

So we now move to the level of imagination, sharing three images of worship that express in figurative language what we have been describing with maps and terms. We hope that these images will inspire your own visions, which in turn will renew your energy for the hard work of worship analysis and liturgical planning.

### Image One: Balanced Diet

A figure with a banana for a torso and bananas for arms and legs was eating a banana. Another figure with an ice cream cone for a body and a scoop of ice cream for a head was eating an ice cream cone. Above the first grade bulletin board was printed in bold letters, "National Nutrition Week: You are what you eat." The children's naïvete had captured the truth of the dietary maxim with a clarity that we adults seldom achieve.

We are what we feed upon. That is why Paul urged his friends, "all that is true, all that is noble, all that is just and pure, all that is lovable and attractive, whatever is excellent and admirable—fill your thoughts with these things" (Philippians 4:8 REB). The church becomes what it consumes. The church gathers to feed upon Christ in song and prayer, in proclaimed word and sacrament.

Like any diet, the church's diet needs to be balanced. If all we sing are metrical hymns, our corporate spirituality will have a high sense of structure, but will lack the fluidity of chant and spiritual and folk music. On the other hand, if we limit ourselves to flowing forms while neglecting the heritage of metrical psalmody and hymnody, then we will lack that sense of dependable pulse that reassures us by its historical connections and its familiar cadences.

Healthy congregational song requires a balanced diet: we are what we sing.

### Image Two: Open Windows

In our part of the country at least half of the year is spent with storm windows and doors sealed shut. In the course of the winter I (Tom) sometimes turn off the heat and open the window in my study. I am glad to wear an extra sweater simply to have fresh air in the room. And I understand from friends in the Deep South that they go through a reverse process, often longing for the scent of earth and flowers in their air-conditioned buildings. How good it is when that time of year comes when we can throw open our windows and feel the air sweeping through the house.

The church's prayer easily grows musty. We are preparing a service of worship. Time is pressing upon us. We know people have come to expect what "we always do." So we just fill in the blank spots in the bulletin and place our denomination's recent liturgical resources on the shelf. We leave untouched the fitting words that would open the congregation to a fresh burst of the Spirit and lift them to visions not yet seen.

It would take so much time and energy and leadership from the musician, pastor, and worship committee working together to introduce the new material. And then it would probably require some initial readjustment, just as the temperature of the room changes when we throw open the windows. But to feel the fresh wind of the Spirit blowing through our congregation would make all the extra preparation worthwhile.

### *Image Three: From Spring to Ocean*

As a boy I used to walk in the rolling countryside to a spring that began in the hills above my home. Its small, but constant, trickle formed a rill, which fed into a creek, which ran through a cow pasture where it gathered to Brookwood Stream, which flowed into Otsego Lake, the source of the Susquehanna River, which widens into Chesapeake Bay before it empties into the Atlantic Ocean. The first time I saw the bay and the ocean, the spring and the rill flashed in my memory. Where does one end and the other begin? The ocean is in the spring, and the spring is in the ocean.

Tradition is like that. The source is in the flow, and the flow is in the source. Congregational worship may take new forms, changing the shape of the culture through which it runs and at the same time being changed by the culture. The taste of its originating spring is the same: the persistent need of the heart to break forth in prayer and song for the joy of being and to give thanks and praise for what God has done for us in Christ. But to stop only at the ancient wells of inspiration, or to settle only farther down the stream, with the words and music of our own time, is to reduce tradition to a still and stagnant pond. Healthy congregational worship is always in touch with tradition, from the spring to the ocean, from the past to the present.

Maintain a balanced diet.

Open the windows.

Travel the whole river.

And your church at worship will sense "the depth of the riches and wisdom and knowledge of God" (Romans 11:33*a*).

# CHAPTER

# Strategies for Change
## *Working With the Tribes*

In recent years there has been a growing amount of research and literature that comes under the general heading of "congregational studies." Scholars have drawn on the social sciences to try to understand the way congregations work as a system. For example, the Center for Parish Development in Chicago has combined organizational analysis, especially the work of Rensis Likert, with theological reflection to probe the relationship between a congregation and its leaders, and the Alban Institute has used an array of sociological and psychodynamic approaches to understand the healthy and ineffectual functioning of parishes. More recently the Grubb Institute, which was first based in Great Britain and from whose work we drew the theory of oscillation (chapter 3, page 102), has established operations in the United States. All of these groups provide regular conferences and consultations to examine the way churches and their leaders work together.[1]

## *Realism About Tribal Politics*

Although congregational studies as a field is broader than the liturgical life of a congregation, all of the research indicates that change in any one arena of the church's life will have consequences for the others. Therefore, the resistance or acceptance that greets the reform of worship may be fed by factors that are not purely liturgical. Perhaps people love hearing the new bell choir, but feel obligated to resist because they favored spending the money on something else that they considered more essential. Perhaps one group is wholeheartedly in favor of the new Communion service because it is upsetting to the clique that holds control of all the visible roles in church.

Part of changing worship is being realistic about church politics. Because worship is a congregation's most regular public event and because it is an experience in which meaning and relationships are symbolically enacted, it is a meeting ground for the forces that are at work throughout the church's life.

If, for example, the pastor feels threatened by increasing lay participation in the operation of the church, then conflict over worship may express the struggle for power more than the decision about what is liturgically appropriate. The pastor may be fighting to hang onto the last well-defined piece of clerical authority. In such situations, no amount of appeal to principles will be sufficient for settling the dispute. The maps and terms we have outlined are essential to a healthy worship life, but in order to use them effectively they must be understood by a group of leaders who can interpret them to the congregation at large.

That is why we believe so strongly in the importance of worship committees consisting of the pastor(s), chief musician(s), and a cross-section of the congregation. When such committees meet regularly, and when they expend the time and effort necessary to master the principles we have outlined, the authority of the pastor actually increases because it is no longer seen as the arbitrary expression of power. The worship committee becomes a working group that can interpret to others in the congregation the purpose and meaning of liturgical reforms.

Sometimes pastors and lay leaders are reluctant to establish such a committee because they see that it will require significant energy to get the group underway. They are correct about this; it will demand much effort. But over the long run there will be less energy lost to the wrangling and misunderstanding that arise when there is no established group process to give continuing attention to the congregation's worship life.

## Getting a Worship Committee Started

When a committee first meets, a good place to begin is to give members an opportunity to tell about their background as worshipers—to identify the tribal memories and customs that people bring from their past, especially from their childhood. These memories run deep in the blood, and they often exercise a hidden power over people's responses to worship because they have never been brought to awareness. Here is a list of questions that we have asked workshop participants:

• What are your earliest memories of worship?
• In what geographic area was the church located?
• Name three of the most common hymns or pieces of congregational music that you recall.
• What did the church of your childhood look like? Were there any particular windows or symbols that persist in your mind's eye?
• What do you remember about Christmas, Easter, and any other special celebrations?
• Are there any particular songs, rituals, or prayers that you associate with significant memories of faith, hope, support, empowerment?

To recall the past experiences of committee members in this manner can help us understand the richness of memory and emotive material that the entire congregation brings to the act of worship.

## Identifying the Tribes' Common Vision

The memory of the past is not in itself an adequate basis for directing the worship life of a congregation. The Center for Parish Development has discovered that one of the most decisive factors in the vitality of any church is whether or not it has a vision of the future and leaders who can help the congregation achieve that vision. Building upon an exercise from the Center's work on leadership skills, we have often asked conference participants, working alone or in groups of three or four, to draw their ideal vision of their church at worship. We ask people to use no words and not to worry about their artistic excellence. They may use any symbols they want, and the drawing can be done as an abstraction or a "realistic" picture. Once the pictures are finished people have an opportunity to interpret their drawing to others, and then to hear from the group what it sees in the picture that may have eluded its creator(s).

The instruction not to use words is *very* important. Because most of the people involved are frequently engaged in conversation about their church, they fall into certain verbal ruts that define their perceptions and understandings. To move from a verbal to a visual form of communication often elicits from them expressions and patterns that are blocked by their normal way of talking about things.

If people have a leadership role, we ask them to include themselves in the drawing as a way of helping them to think about how they relate to the congregation.

Most participants carry out the exercise with insight and imagination, except that they frequently find it difficult to avoid the use of words and impossible to indicate the position of the leader. This is significant data. It reveals how much people think of worship as something that is spoken—rather than symbolized and enacted—and how problematic the role of leader has become. How do we visualize the role of leader in an age that is suspicious of leaders and in a church that wants to stress that worship is the action of the entire congregation?

A pastor who was feeling the tension of these questions once called me to lead a retreat with the church's ruling body. Five of the visions that people drew at that retreat are found here. There were seventeen in all, but I am providing the five that took center stage during the group discussion. All of the pictures were done with felt-tip markers and were bolder and more striking than what I have recorded here.

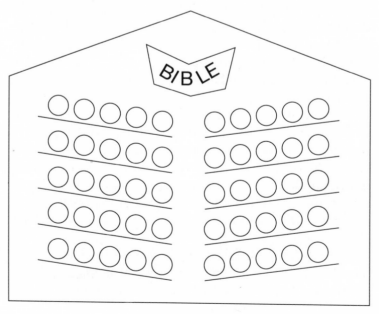

Vision # 1

Vision #1 was drawn by the group most disgruntled with the current pastor and the current lay leadership of the church. Notice that there is no pastor behind the pulpit! Their ideal was a full church listening to the Word of God, which for them meant "preaching straight from the Bible." Using our earlier maps we can see that this vision highly favors structure.

Members of the larger group found the absence of windows and awareness of the world outside the church "suffocating." Some people said that as much as they wanted to hear from the Bible, the Bible was not adequate in itself since they were facing issues that were never foreseen by the scriptural writers, such as how to interpret the mass media to their children and medical ethics decisions regarding abortion and the treatment of the terminally ill.

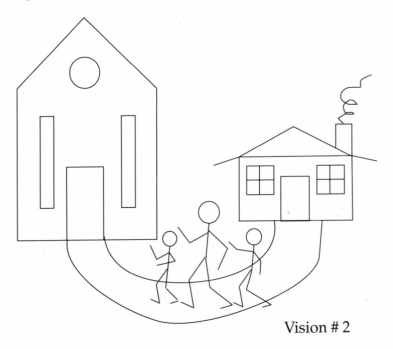

Vision # 2

Vision #2 was done by a number of people who were above all concerned with the breakdown of family life in the community and among members of the congregation. They wanted a worship life that would strengthen families and would welcome "any forms of worship that would appeal across the generations."

All the groups, including #1, agreed that this was an important goal for the church's ministry, but many found the vision too simplistic, as if the church had some precast answer to the social complexities of families coming apart.

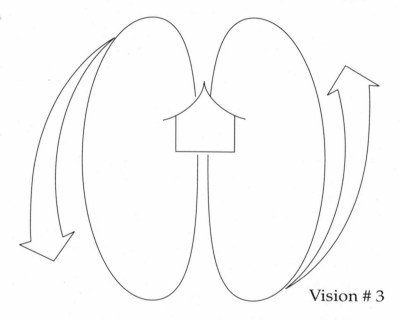

Vision # 3

Vision #3 locates the church at the center of what looks like two lungs. The church is to be a "power pump" that would send more and more energy for mission out into the world, represented by the circulating arrows.

When people responded with a sense of exhaustion to this drawing, its creator acknowledged her own exhaustion with the words, "I am a worn-out social activist, worn-out from trying to get this church caring about problems of the city."

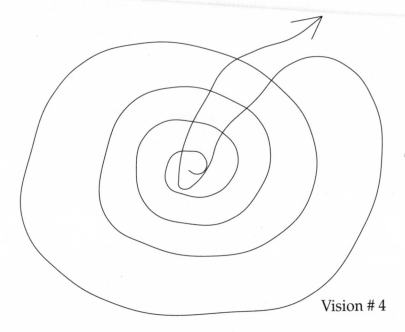

Vision # 4

Vision #4 brought sighs of admiration from the group for its dramatic use of many colors so that it looked like a rainbow that had coiled upon itself. Its creator explained that when she thought of the church at its best she thought of its sacred choral concerts featuring Handel's *Messiah* or Mendelssohn's *Elijah*. These were more than concerts for her. They were occasions of prayer when she went "down deep into my soul" (represented by the line that hooks below the center of the swirl) and then "came back up reaching toward God" (the arrow arching toward heaven).

The creators of vision #1 were disturbed by vision #4: "It's just an experience. It is not clear about the Bible or

Jesus." The conflict was between pure structure and pure anti-structure. The other members of the group saw this, and the visualization of the differences set them on a creative discussion about how they would bring these together so that the church would receive an appropriate balance.

Vision # 5

Notice that the role of leader is missing in all of these diagrams even though many of these people were counted among the church's leaders. It was not until vision #5 was presented that the leader image was made explicit. This is the pastor's vision. It was based on a Bible study that we did on the first day of the retreat about the healing of the paralytic whose friends lowered him to Jesus through a hole in the roof. In the pastor's vision we are looking down and seeing the head of the pastor at the center of the diagram. Each of the figures extending from the center is a person on a stretcher. The outer end of each stretcher is carried by someone else, but the inside of all the stretchers is carried by the pastor alone, hence the circling lines around the pastor to indicate that he is continually turning to try to handle all the stretchers at once!

The pastor felt trapped because if he walked off with any one stretcher—that is to say, if he followed the direction of any one group in the church—he would have to drop the others. Once the pastor identified his dilemma, a number of persons in the group began to analyze how their own visions were not only putting him in a bind, but were also resulting in institutional stasis. They then began to identify in each vision what it was that they could affirm and what kind of vision they could agree to in common.

Most of them were able to begin to move toward a broader and more flexible vision of their church and particularly of its worship. But the people who drew vision #1 were not satisfied. They had a need for high structure, which could not be reconciled with the hopes of the larger group. Some of these people eventually found another church home, but others became excited about the new vision that emerged and stayed on.

It is important to note in this story that the process could not accommodate every need and every vision. The realization that any one church cannot be all things to all people is often painful, especially if we care about the community and are willing to bend to keep it from coming apart.

Although any church will have defining limits to its vision, our experience indicates that congregations are capable of a higher degree of inclusivity and diversity than they think. These possibilities often go unrealized because the necessary background work of interpreting tribe to tribe has not been done.

We need to understand that this interpretive task is a large part of what it means to be the body of Christ, to live the gospel of reconciliation. The church's proclamation of a global vision of peace and justice sounds hollow when the church is at war itself about how to pray. Much of the violence and hatred that tear the world apart is "religious" in nature; that is, its roots are in deeply held convictions about the ultimate nature of things. Our tribe is right and your tribe is wrong.

Thus the process we have described for achieving vital worship in a pluralistic church can be viewed as a kind of training for peacemaking in the world. Taking the time to listen to the tribal customs of others and to work toward a common vision can teach us what is actually involved in being ambassadors of reconciliation in the larger world (2 Corinthians 5:18ff.).

## Reconciling the Tribes as a Form of Spirituality

We have no illusion that any of what we have described is easy. We have had our own struggles to understand songs, rituals, and ways of prayer that were, on our first exposure, alien and upsetting to what we considered the "right" way to worship.

I (Tom) can recall, for example, when I first started teaching in an ecumenical seminary and attended worship in a number of traditions that were strange to me. My first reaction to many services was a swift judgment of favor or dislike. Since we worshiped three times a week, this soon began to exhaust my spiritual energies. I decided that I had to take some action to change the automatic internal processing of my heart and mind. So I began to pray the following prayer every time I entered the chapel:

Holy Spirit,
Help me to withhold judgment
of what is strange and new to me.
Use this service of worship
to deepen my belief in God,
to expand my understanding of the gospel,
to strengthen my bonds with all people
and to serve more faithfully Jesus Christ,
in whose name I pray, Amen.

For several months I prayed this prayer at the beginning of every service. Then one day I realized I had ceased praying it. I no longer had to offer the prayer because the Spirit had answered my request so that I was able to give myself to a multiplicity of ways of worshiping God.

This does not mean that I lost all my critical faculties or that I found every service moving. The principles we have described in this book hold up across denominational lines, and services that achieved no appropriate balance of structure and anti-structure or that appealed to only one personality type were as dissatisfying to those who led them as to the people in the pew.

As the Spirit answered my prayer, I came to realize that vital worship is not the exclusive property of any one tradition. The prayer connected my internal processing to structures of meaning and praise that were preserved by other communities of faith and that represented truth that is larger than the perimeters of my private experience.

We have now worked with enough churches and leaders around the country to see that this story is not at all unique. We are glad to say that there are many others who in their own way have offered the same prayer to the Spirit. A desire for openness to the traditions of others is more widespread than our fragmented society may lead us to believe. What we are talking about here is an attitude of the heart, a posture of the soul toward other tribes who seek to worship God in ways different from our own.

We believe that this attitude of the heart represents a form of spirituality without which all the theories and terms of liturgical study are to no avail. Although many people thirst earnestly to acquire "spirituality," others disparage their quest as either mindless or leading to a privatized inwardness. However, the potential for vagueness and narcissism is minimized when spirituality grows out of the search for a renewal of the community's worship through the reconciliation of the church's many tribes. Such renewal does include attention to one's interior personal state:

> Holy Spirit,
> Help *me* to withhold judgment
> of what is strange and new to *me*.

But this interiority begins by recognizing the inadequacy of myself. What is strange and new to me is not strange and new to the others who worship that way nor is it strange and new to the Spirit who is moving through their hearts and delighting in their song and prayer.

We are encouraging an attitude of heart that seeks openness to others in order to strengthen our bonds with all people and to serve Jesus Christ more faithfully. Thus the spirituality we describe does not eschew personal prayer or attention to one's internal processes, but it frames those in the setting of the larger community of faith and the many tribes that are different from our own.

Such a spirituality is in part what the apostle Paul develops in his extended argument about the nature of the church and its gifts in 1 Corinthians chapters 12, 13, and 14. In our experience people often isolate chapter 12 or chapter 13 independently of each other, and they forget chapter 14 altogether. But the three chapters form a unit, an extended reflection on the nature of the church.

Chapter 12 deals with the church as the body of Christ. Chapter 13 is the famous passage about love. When it is read by itself we are apt to distort it into the description of love as a feeling in the heart extended to another individual. But it is the centerpiece of an argument that extends into chapter 14, which stresses again and again that the crucial test of the various ways we worship is whether or not they build up the church (1 Corinthians 14:3, 5, 12, 26).

The context of chapter 13 suggests that one of the things Paul has in mind when he writes the following words is how people will treat each other in dealing with their differences over worship—differences that were threatening to tear apart the church at Corinth: "Love is patient; love is kind; love is not envious or boastful or arrogant or rude. It does not insist on its own way; it is not irritable or resentful" (1 Corinthians 13:4-5).

The spirituality we are describing involves the living out of these words in the ordering and practice of our liturgical life. We know that is not any easier nowadays than it was when Paul was writing to Corinth or centuries before his time when the tribes went up to Jerusalem "to give thanks to the name of the LORD."

We opened this book recalling that scholars did not know whether the psalmist was describing idealized or actual practice. But there is every reason to believe that it was primarily an unrealized vision that the psalmist describes. For there are many other passages where the tribes, far from showing patient love toward each other, were cursing and fighting one another. Genesis 49, which is written in the form of a blessing by Jacob, is filled with hostile and disparaging statements about certain tribes while praising others, statements that were probably part of the common prejudice held by some tribes against the others:

Simeon and Levi are brothers;
    weapons of violence are their swords.
May I never come into their council;
    may I not be joined to their company—
for in their anger they killed men,
    and at their whim they
        hamstrung oxen.
Cursed be their anger, for it is fierce,
    and their wrath, for it is cruel!
I will divide them in Jacob,
    and scatter them in Israel.

Judah, your brothers shall praise you;
    your hand shall be on the neck
      of your enemies;
    your father's sons shall bow
      down before you.
(Genesis 49:5-8)

Ancient rivalries have plagued the community of faith in every generation. The Samaritan woman at the well reveals some of the divisions that kept people apart in Jesus' day. She tells him: "'Our ancestors worshiped on this mountain, but you say that the place where people must worship is in Jerusalem'" (John 4:20).

When we recall that John wrote his Gospel for a community of Christians and that he often shaped his stories to make a sermonic point, then it is not unlikely that John is using the exchange between the Samaritan woman and Christ to clarify a principle for the community's worship life. Christ does not get entangled in the details of who is right and who is wrong, the Samaritan liturgists or the Jerusalem liturgists. Instead he articulates the deeper principle that applies to all groups—the Samaritans, the worshipers in Jerusalem, the members of John's community, and those of us who continue to read his Gospel in our own day: "'But the hour is coming, and is now here, when the true worshipers will worship the Father in spirit and truth, for the Father seeks such as these to worship him. God is spirit, and those who worship him must worship in spirit and truth'" (John 4:23-24).

To worship in "spirit and truth" is the attitude of the heart, the posture of the soul that we are describing as an authentic spirituality for the revitalization of the church's corporate prayer. Such spiritual discipline, as the stories of this book and your own experience reveal, is demanding. It is not something that sells easily or that provides instant liturgical success. But we are sustained in the rigors of this discipline by Christ's words that God is seeking people who want to worship in "spirit and truth." This means that the entire burden is not on us. God is looking for us! And when our seeking and God's seeking meet, then the psalmist's vision moves from ideal to actuality; the tribes gather together to give thanks to the name of the Lord and to pray for the peace of the household of God.

# APPENDIX

# Pastor,* Lead Our Circle Dance

(tune: Rockwell)

For the Rt. Reverend Hays Rockwell, on the occasion of his Ordination and Consecration
as Bishop Coadjutor of the Diocese of Missouri, March 2, 1991.

THOMAS H. TROEGER

CAROL DORAN

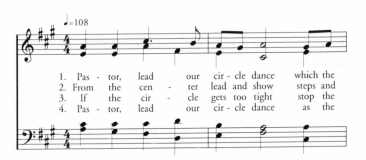

1. Pas - tor, lead our cir - cle dance which the
2. From the cen - ter lead and show steps and
3. If the cir - cle gets too tight stop the
4. Pas - tor, lead our cir - cle dance as the

1. Spir - it has be - gun, Help us hand in
2. leaps we nev - er tried, Then al - low the
3. dance and don't be - gin till our o - pen
4. Spir - it leads and calls till the cir - cle's

1. hand ad - vance, show us how to move as
2. dance to flow, danc- ing with us side by
3. hands in - vite all whom Je - sus wel - comes
4. whole ex- panse moves be- yond our bounds and

* Bishop, Deacon, Rector, Elder, Teacher, etc.

Based on 2 Samuel 6:14-15

1. one.     Some    de-mand a   driv-ing beat,
2. side.      Let    each danc - er   take a   turn,
3. in.        For    the dance of   faith be-longs
4. walls     And    we dance with   dis-tant suns

**Broadening**

1. oth-ers   ask to slow the pace.      Teach us how to
2. danc-ing   in the cen-ter free       so that all can
3. to the strang-ers in   the street,     and   we need their
4. danc-ing   in the dark a - bove,      danc-ing as cre -

*ritard.*

1. bend and meet    our con - flict-ed needs     with   grace.
2. teach and learn   what our   cir - cle dance    could   be.
3. steps and songs   for the   dance to   be     com - plete.
4. a - tion runs     on the   en - er - gies     of   love.

From *New Hymns for the Life of the Church,*
© 1990 Oxford University Press. Reproduced by permission.

# NOTES

## 1. Trouble at the Table: The Crisis in Worship

1. Paul Westermeyer, "The Practical Life of the Church Musician," in Christian Century, September 13-20, 1989, p. 812.

2. J. W. Rogerson and J. W. McKay, The Cambridge Bible Commentary on the New English Bible, Psalms 101-150 (Cambridge: Cambridge University Press, 1977), p. 118.

3. Harper's Bible Dictionary, p. 783.

4. Center for Parish Development, Leadership Skills for Effective Ministry, manual and laboratory offered by the center, Chicago, Ill., 1983.

5. Lawrence A. Hoffman, The Art of Public Prayer: Not for Clergy Only (Washington, D.C.: Pastoral Press, 1988), p. 174.

6. See Marjorie Proctor-Smith, In Her Own Rite: Constructing Feminist Liturgical Tradition (Nashville: Abingdon Press, 1990). We are indebted for this insight and question to Proctor-Smith's entire first chapter, which is entitled after a line from Adrienne Rich, "Are they true for us?"

7. The United Methodist Hymnal: Book of United Methodist Worship (Nashville: The United Methodist Publishing House, 1989), no. 57.

8. The Hymnal 1982 (New York: The Church Hymnal Corporation, 1985), no. 493.

9. Hoffman, The Art of Public Prayer, p. 56.

10. J. G. Davies, ed., The Westminster Dictionary of Worship (Philadelphia: The Westminster Press, 1976), p. 222.

11. Robert Bellah, et al., Habits of the Heart: Individualism and Commitment in American Life (Berkeley: University of California, 1985), p. 232. The study cited is from Dean R. Hoge, Converts, Dropouts, Returnees: A Study of Religious Change Among Catholics (New York: Pilgrim Press, 1981), p. 167.

12. Neil Postman, Amusing Ourselves to Death: Public Discourse in the Age of Show Business (New York: Viking, 1985), p. 87.

13. Ibid., pp. 87 and 92.

14. Bellah, et al., Habits of the Heart, p. 276.

15. Michael B. Aune, "Worship in an Age of Subjectivism Revisited," Worship 65, no. 3 (May 1991): 236.

16. Thomas H. Troeger, "Make Our Church One Joyful Choir" (New York: Oxford University Press, 1991), unpublished hymn.

17. Aune, "Worship in an Age of Subjectivism Revisited," 236-37.

18. See Richard Ward, Speaking from the Heart: Preaching with Passion (Nashville: Abingdon Press, 1992).

19. Rogerson and McKay, Psalms 101-150, p. 118.

20. Ibid., pp. 118-19.

21. James Dallen, "Liturgy and Justice for All," Worship 65, no. 4 (July 1991): 290.

22. In their instruction manual, Leadership Skills for Effective Ministry, there is a step-by-step process that leads to drawing an image of the church that includes showing ourselves in our usual leadership behavior (module 2, topic 1, p. 7). We will examine this exercise in more detail in chapter 4.

23. See, for example, the following works. In linguistics: George Lakoff and Mark Johnson, Metaphors We Live By (Chicago: The University of Chicago Press, 1980); Frank Burch Brown, Transfiguration: Poetic Metaphor and the Languages of Religious Belief (Chapel Hill, N.C.: The University of North Carolina Press, 1983). In theology: David Tracy, The Analogical Imagination: Christian Theology and the Culture of Pluralism (New York: Crossroad Publishing, 1981); Sallie McFague, Metaphorical Theology: Models of God in Religious Language (Philadelphia: Fortress Press, 1982).

24. Instead of the word pastor you can use any other appropriate title of two syllables with the accent on the first beat: e.g., Bishop, Deacon, Rector, Elder, Teacher, and so on.

25. Carol Doran and Thomas H. Troeger, New Hymns for the Life of the Church: To Make Our Prayer and Music One (New York: Oxford University Press, 1991), no. 12.

26. Dallen, "Liturgy and Justice for All," 302.

27. Elaine Scarry, The Body in Pain: The Making and Unmaking of the World (New York: Oxford University Press, 1985), p. 7.

## 2. Worship and Music: Hearing Again the Harmony of the Spheres

1. John Hollander, The Untuning of the Sky: Ideas of Music in English Poetry, 1500-1700 (New York: W. W. Norton & Company, 1991), pp. 11-12.

2. Gunther Schuller, Musings: The Musical Worlds of Gunther Schuller, A Collection of His Writings (New York: Oxford University Press, 1986), p. 259.

3. W. A. Mathieu, The Listening Book: Discovering Your Own Music (Boston & London: Shambhala, 1991), p. 37. Emphasis added.

4. David R. Newman, Worship as Praise and Empowerment (New York: The Pilgrim Press, 1988), pp. 12-13.

5. Robin A. Leaver, "The Theological Character of Music in Worship," in Duty & Delight: Routley Remembered, Robin A. Leaver, James H. Litton, Carlton R. Young, eds. (Carol Stream, Ill.: Hope Publishing Company, 1985), p. 49.

6. We are indebted here to Richard Gudgeon, whose unpublished D.Min. thesis on Martin Luther's pastoral use of music, in the Colgate Rochester Divinity

School library, extensively documents references from Martin Luther's writing on the relationship of music and theology.

7. Luther's Works, vol. 53, Liturgy and Hymns (Philadelphia: Fortress Press, 1965), p. 323.

8. Mathieu, The Listening Book, p. 5.

9. Ibid., p. 33.

10. Fred Pratt Green, "When in Our Music God Is Glorified," in The Hymns and Ballads of Fred Pratt Green (Carol Stream, Ill.: Hope Publishing Company, 1982), p. 51.

11. Alice Parker, Melodious Accord: Good Singing in Church (Chicago: Liturgy Training Publications, 1991); and James Rawlings Sydnor, Hymns and Their Uses (Carol Stream, Ill.: Agape, 1982).

12. Sally Belfrage, Freedom Summer (Charlottesville, Va.: University Press of Virginia, 1990), as quoted in "Noted with Pleasure," The New York Times Book Review, November 4, 1990, p. 43.

13. James Anderson Winn, Unsuspected Eloquence: A History of the Relations Between Poetry and Music (New Haven: Yale University Press, 1981), p. 4.

14. Ibid., p. 13.

15. Hollander, The Untuning of the Sky, p. 34.

16. Winn, Unsuspected Eloquence, p. 35.

17. Ibid., p. 94.

18. The Confessions of St. Augustine, trans. John K. Ryan (Garden City, N.Y.: Image Books, 1960), pp. 261-62. Emphasis added.

19. Johannes Ruber, Bach and the Heavenly Choir, trans. Maurice Michael (Cleveland: The World Publishing Company, 1956), pp. 125-26.

20. Ibid., p. 128.

21. Sidney Lanier, Music and Poetry: Essays upon Some Aspects and Interrelations of the Two Arts (New York: Greenwood Press Publishers, 1970), p. 18.

22. Rodney S. Lightfoote, A History of Seneca Presbyterian Church "Old Number Nine," written on the occasion of the 175th anniversary, 1807-1982, privately published, p. 25.

23. Hollander, The Untuning of the Sky, pp. 104-5.

24. We know of at least the following new hymnals that include "Jesus, Remember Me": The Presbyterian Hymnal: Hymns, Psalms and Spiritual Songs (Louisville: Westminster/John Knox Press, 1990), no. 599; The United Methodist Hymnal (Nashville: The United Methodist Publishing House, 1989), no. 488; The Worshipping Church (1990), no. 822; Worship III, A Hymnal and Service Book for Roman Catholics (Chicago: GIA Publishers, 1986), no. 423.

25. In chapter 3 we will be discussing theories that will provide a fuller analysis of this experience, especially the material on the theory of oscillation.

26. Virginia Woolf, The Essays of Virginia Woolf, vol. 1, ed. Andrew McNeillie (San Diego: Harcourt Brace Jovanovich, 1986), p. 29.

27. Thomas H. Troeger, unpublished poem, copyright 1991 (New York: Oxford University Press).

28. Anne Sexton, "Music Swims Back to Me." In The Bedlam and Part Way Back (Boston: Houghton Mifflin, 1960).

29. Walter Chalmers Smith, "Immortal, Invisible, God Only Wise," The United Methodist Hymnal (Nashville: The United Methodist Publishing House, 1989), no. 103.

30. Music in Catholic Worship, III, "The Place of Music in the Celebration: Music Serves the Expression of Faith" (Bishops' Committee on the Liturgy, 1967), no. 23. Emphasis added.

31. Leo Sowerby, Ideals in Church Music (Greenwich, Conn.: Seabury Press, 1956), p. 6.

32. American Organist, October 1989, p. 112.

33. Cynthia Serjak, RSM, Music and the Cosmic Dance (Washington, D.C.: The Pastoral Press, 1987), p. 44.

34. Schuller, "The State of Our Art," in Musings, p. 259.

35. On the necessity of memory to the church's identity and mission, see Johann Baptist Metz, Faith in History and Society: Toward a Practical Fundamental Theology, trans. David Smith (New York: The Seabury Press, 1980), pp. 184ff.

36. Quoted by Michael Edwards in Towards a Christian Poetics (Grand Rapids: Eerdmans Publishing Company, 1984), p. 127.

37. Virgil C. Funk, "Reflections," Pastoral Music Notebook 8 (May 1984): 4.

38. Available from Buffalo Chapter, American Guild of Organists, Dean Harold Pysher, P.O. Box 233, Williamsville, NY 14221.

39. Futures Commission Meeting of the Association of Anglican Musicians, March 3, 1982.

## 3. Maps and Images: Giving Shape to the Yearnings of the Heart

1. See Urban Holmes III, Ministry and Imagination (New York: Seabury Press, 1981).

2. Ibid., p. 135. We have adapted the diagram in the light of our workshops and classes.

3. David R. Newman, Worship as Praise and Empowerment (New York: The Pilgrim Press, 1988), p. 19. Emphasis added.

4. Two recent books that trace some of the most significant chapters in the history of the relationship between art and Western Christian worship are: Gregor T. Goethals, The Electronic Golden Calf: Images, Religion, and the Making of Meaning (Cambridge, Mass.: Cowley Publications, 1990); and Janet R. Walton, Art and Worship: A Vital Connection (Wilmington, Del.: Michael Glazier, Inc., 1988). Both books are helpful in describing not only the history, but also the present implications for the church's life.

5. Margaret Miles, Image as Insight: Visual Understanding in Western Christianity and Secular Culture (Boston: Beacon Press, 1985), p. 98. We are indebted to Miles for much of our discussion here, particularly chapter 5, "Vision and Sixteenth Century Protestant and Roman Catholic Reforms."

6. Cited in ibid., p. 103.

7. We are indebted to a former colleague, James B. Ashbrook, for this phrase.

8. George Arthur Buttrick, ed. The Interpreter's Dictionary of the Bible, vol. 2 (Nashville: Abingdon Press, 1962), p. 549.

9. Charles J. Keating, Who We Are Is How We Pray: Matching Personality and Spirituality (Mystic, Conn.: Twenty-third Publications, 1988), p. 9.

10. Chester P. Michael and Marie C. Norrisey, Prayer and Temperament: Different Prayer Forms for Different Personality Types (Charlottesville, Va.: The Open Door, 1984), p. 16.

11. Keating, Who We Are Is How We Pray, p. 4.

12. Goethals, The Electronic Golden Calf, pp. 198ff.

13. Ibid., pp. 124ff.

14. Buttrick, ed., The Interpreter's Dictionary of the Bible, vol. 3, pp. 344-45.

15. We are indebted to Aidan Kavanagh of Yale University, who shared this with us from a file he has kept of such examples.

16. Amos N. Wilder, Grace Confounding: Poems (Philadelphia: Fortress Press, 1972), p. ix.

## 4. Stategies for Change: Working with the Tribes

1. If you want to pursue this research, you can write to the following addresses requesting a bibliography of their publications, as well as the schedule of their workshops and conferences, which are held throughout the continental United States so that travel costs can be kept within reason.

The Center for Parish Development
5407 S. University Avenue
Chicago, Illinois 60615

The Alban Institute, Inc.
Mount St. Alban
Washington, D.C. 20016

The Grubb Institute
1900 L Street NW, Suite 500
Washington, D.C. 20036

In the case study presented in this last chapter, we have drawn heavily on the Center's studies of leadership and on the Alban Institute's work on conflict management.